Non-Anxious Churches

Non-Anxious Churches

Finding the Way of Jesus for Pastors and Churches Today

MARK KNIGHT

Foreword by Mark Novak

RESOURCE *Publications* • Eugene, Oregon

NON-ANXIOUS CHURCHES
Finding the Way of Jesus for Pastors and Churches Today

Copyright © 2022 Mark Knight. All rights reserved. Except for brief quotations in critical publications or reviews, no part of this book may be reproduced in any manner without prior written permission from the publisher. Write: Permissions, Wipf and Stock Publishers, 199 W. 8th Ave., Suite 3, Eugene, OR 97401.

Resource Publications
An Imprint of Wipf and Stock Publishers
199 W. 8th Ave., Suite 3
Eugene, OR 97401

www.wipfandstock.com

PAPERBACK ISBN: 978-1-6667-3660-1
HARDCOVER ISBN: 978-1-6667-9518-9
EBOOK ISBN: 978-1-6667-9519-6

JANUARY 14, 2022 8:32 AM

All Scripture quotations, unless otherwise indicated, are taken from the Holy Bible, New International Version®, NIV®. Copyright ©1973, 1978, 1984, 2011 by Biblica, Inc.™ Used by permission of Zondervan. All rights reserved worldwide. www.zondervan.comThe "NIV" and "New International Version" are trademarks registered in the United States Patent and Trademark Office by Biblica, Inc.™

Contents

Foreword by Mark Novak | vii

INTRODUCTION | ix

Chapter 1   HOW DID WE GET HERE? | 1

Chapter 2   ANXIOUS PASTORS | 8

Chapter 3   AMBITIOUS PASTORS | 15

Chapter 4   ANXIOUS CHURCHES FUELED BY PERFORMANCE | 28

Chapter 5   ANXIOUS CHURCHES FUELED BY FEAR | 38

Chapter 6   NON-ANXIOUS PASTORS | 45

Chapter 7   NON-ANXIOUS CHURCHES | 61

Chapter 8   NON-ANXIOUS LEADERSHIP | 77

Chapter 9   PASTORING ANXIOUS PEOPLE | 91

Chapter 10   BECOMING A NON-ANXIOUS CHURCH | 109

EPILOGUE | 128

Appendix 1: Non-Anxious Church Quiz | 131

Acknowledgments | 137

About Mark Knight | 139

Bibliography | 141

Foreword
by Mark Novak

I REMEMBER DISTINCTLY A late-night text from a church chairman that read; "Please call me ASAP. We just discovered our pastor has had a moral failure." As shocking as this message may seem, this text wasn't uncommon for me. I received lots of calls and texts similar to this one, and those conversations started the process of recovery for many folks under my care. For seventeen years as a Conference Superintendent and Executive Minister for Develop Leaders for the Evangelical Covenant Church, I walked folks through our credentialing process, continuing education, and care process in a case of moral or ethical failure.

I learned firsthand that isolation, fatigue, and a lack of affirmation are only a few of the reasons pastors make life-altering choices. So many told me if they knew then what they know now, they would not have been in their situation. What they came to know in a new way was the deep work of self-care and a deeper intimacy with Jesus.

This is why I am writing the forward for this book. After forty-plus years in ministry working directly with churches, pastors, and leaders, I want people to understand that there is a different way to lead a church or ministry. There is a different way to live life. If we allow what Mark Knight has put together to permeate our lives, our ministries will be environments where people thrive and find health. You will not find a formula in this book, but you will catch a vision for a deeper, more authentic life, and ministry. A non-anxious leader provides the perfect framework for trust, which is the key to leadership in any context. It seeks to build up those around us, and invites us to ask a different set of questions regarding success and significance.

Foreword

I invite you to read with a mindset of hope, dreaming about how to be a non-anxious leader in your context! Forgive yourself for past failures and give yourself the freedom to imagine a new way to take people into a deeper and more fulfilling relationship with God. Enjoy this read because the Church needs leaders with a different set of markers for success, ones more than attendance numbers and budget lines. We need to restructure our lives to journey with people graciously and genuinely through all of life.

Enjoy!

Rev. Mark A. Novak
Retired Executive Director of Develop Leaders
Evangelical Covenant Church

Introduction

IF I ASKED YOU to imagine an anxious church it wouldn't take a very active imagination to come up with an example. The list of anxiously driven churches is longer than the alternative. The angst that pastors, leaders, and churches feel is on a sliding scale from toxic wasteland and spiritual abuse to simply programmatic but lacking fruit. Anxiousness can cause all manner of issues, as the burnt-out pastor and the consumeristic congregants are just two groups of people devouring the fruit from the systemic anxious tree. The more we learn about narcissism for example, the more we learn it is developed from a deep sense of insecurity and anxiousness.1

On the contrary, if we believe that Christ is with His church then why are we so anxious? The answer to this question is not simple to unwind. Yet, that's what this book seeks to show: the process of unwinding the anxious church — to find our way in sync with the way of Jesus.

The cost is high. The world runs on anxiousness and our neighbors don't need one more option to feel their own inner distress. Instead, our neighbors and congregants need to be shown a way that runs incongruently to the world; the way in which anxiousness is surrendered to Jesus, and everyone is given the option to step into an unshakable kingdom.2 Part of the problem is that many churches don't even realize they are anxious. Anxiousness has a way of masking itself with good intentions and a strong work ethic.

I think as a pastor's kid and a pastor myself, I have discovered this reality but it wasn't until recently that I realized and was able to articulate the vastness of the problem. It seems as if we could rationalize away *those* churches but safely assume the virus of toxic anxiousness hadn't dug into

---

1. DeGroat, *When Narcissism Comes to Church*, 27–28.
2. Hebrews 12:28

Introduction

our church and into our hearts. However, COVID-19 seemed to expose what was lying under the surface.

For me, this realization came a year into the COVID-19 pandemic when I was driving a friend to get his car from a repair shop over an hour away. At the time he was a seminary student, which gave him an extra interest in church culture and church leadership. He was telling me the story about a church in town that changed directions in a 180-degree fashion with regards to the COVID-19 state mandates. It split the staff, the congregation was struggling with how to respond, and the church was reeling in many ways. My friend, always eager to learn from the good, bad, and ugly of church leadership asked me what I thought happened.

I responded with a short answer that led me on the journey to writing this book. I told him; "I think most pastors are more anxious than they let on. There are so many pastors flirting with the edge of burnout and when control is shown as an illusion, there are going to be anxiously made decisions." It wasn't long after this conversation that two more things popped up in my life. First, one of my good friends in ministry submitted his letter of resignation to his church, exhausted from pushing through the toxicity of the church leadership. The other instance was a family member who wasn't wanting to go to a new church on vacation because of how overwhelming it is to be a new person at a church. This family member is a Christian who grew up in church, and yet was anxious about being with another group of fellow Christians.

These are just immediate personal stories. It doesn't take long to accumulate tons of these examples. We could look in the news and see celebrity pastors falling. We could look in our community and see church doors closing. We could talk to young people who grew up in the church and who are no longer interested in attending, and the list goes on. What is going on? I'd like to show how anxiousness has a key role in these situations.

One answer is that anxious churches produce anxious fruit. The anxiety we've grown accustomed to has worked into our vocations and has been allowed to multiply in our discipleship strategies. Anxiety has a way of hiding behind the scenes of our lives. It has a way of being the chameleon in our systems and structures. What looks like energy and momentum may actually be the buzz of an anxiety-producing system.

When churches feel the need to rush to social media for the latest campaign, to take pictures in a way that makes it look like there are more people in the room, when a pastor feels compelled to lie about numbers

Introduction

when standing next to someone they admire or another pastor; these are all tell-tale signs of anxiety-driven ministry.

Anxiety-driven churches can have disastrous results if left unchecked and the cup of anxiety runs over. We need to ask some very big questions about church culture:

- Why are so many pastors failing?
- Why are so many churches losing their young people?
- Why are there so many new prodigals?
- What's the deal with pastors' kids?

We will deal with all of this throughout the book and look at what it means to be an anxiety-driven church versus a non-anxious church. However, before I go much further, I need to say that this book isn't meant to be in any way a "bride-bashing exercise." It's a book that's steeped in love for the church and a great desire to see the church grow into the beautiful and radiant bride described by Revelation 19.

It's easy to see all the problems. It seems as if every other week we have a new public example of ministry failure, whether it be a pastor, speaker, apologist, church leadership, etc. We have seen greed, sexual immorality, power abuse, theological de-railings, and many other examples. There is an obvious problem within the church culture and I would say much of it is anxiousness.

This isn't to say that there aren't toxic people who are taking up humble posts pretending to be shepherds. This is to say that the average church and average pastor lives into and responds to a standard that is molded mostly by anxiety. It may not be stated as such but it is the underlying feeling behind church culture. Maybe better stated, it is the fruit of the westernized version of the church and the fruit is being eaten and reproduced. Anxious fruit. Once again, anxious churches produce anxious fruit.

Let me define what I mean by anxiousness in this book. Anxiety is a complex word in our society. It can mean anything from a fear-laced existence to a stressful situation. It can be chronic or it can be temporary. However, when I think of anxiousness I think of an underlying human condition that comes from a lack of health, this could be internal or external in nature.

Anxiety in this book is defined as a natural discomfort we feel originating from either within or without. We then live into our anxiousness by

Introduction

making decisions to fix this feeling of discomfort or unease. It's important to know that we all have underlying anxiety and it is best seen when we chase after things or make decisions to appease, fulfill, mitigate or compensate for our insecurities. A completely healthy person in all domains: spiritual, emotional, mental, and physical is non-existent, and thus we all operate with some baseline of anxiety as we carve our way through this world.

If we are all living with underlying anxiety and looking for ways to succeed (more money, bigger church, nicer buildings), fulfill (they love me!), or compensate (I'm okay, right?) our way out of it then we can understand these very simple connections. Anxious people become anxious pastors and anxious leaders. These anxious people make anxious decisions to mask the unease or discomfort they feel or have been taught to feel and thus we create anxious churches. These anxious churches then produce anxious fruit.

What's the solution? It's easy to read the solution in this book but it will be tough to live out. It's seeing the story of Martha and Mary not only as a gracious lesson from Jesus to two of his female disciples, but also as a leadership parable.

I assume if you are reading this book that you are familiar with the story of Mary and Martha. This is such an iconic sermon story when we talk about worry, stress, or anxiety. Yet, it's always applied personally and it's always applied to those out there; the finger-pointing to "those anxious people." If you are a pastor or church leader, you've probably rarely thought much about applying that story to how you lead the church and your posture as a leader.

Let's look at the story again but with the idea of church leadership and church culture in the roles of Mary and Martha. The argument of this book is that the majority of the church culture finds an anxious approach to shepherding a church while the posture that Jesus calls us to is the same one as Mary's.

Luke 10:38–42

> As Jesus and his disciples were on their way, he came to a village where a woman named Martha opened her home to him. She had a sister called Mary, who sat at the Lord's feet listening to what he said. But Martha was distracted by all the preparations that had to be made. She came to him and asked, "Lord, don't you care that my sister has left me to do the work by myself? Tell her to help me!" "Martha, Martha," the Lord answered, "you are worried and

upset about many things, but few things are needed—or indeed only one. Mary has chosen what is better, and it will not be taken away from her."

The primary point of the Mary and Martha story is that of discipleship, and we certainly don't want to miss that. In fact, we want to tie it together tighter since the main objective of the church is to make disciples. If disciples are made by sitting at the feet of Jesus and churches are called to make disciples, it seems as if the primary activity of the church should be to sit at the feet of Jesus — not simply as individuals but holistically. The entire church; pastor, elders, leadership, committees, kids ministry, youth ministry, and every other ministry of the church should be sitting at the Lord's feet.

In fact, while we've tried to make this passage about individual discipleship and our quiet time, the posture of sitting at the feet of Jesus is neither meant to be exclusively individual nor is it meant to be regulated to specific areas of our lives. The Scriptures don't have a place for individual Christianity, as if you can be a Christian by yourself, nor does it have a place for discipleship as simply a "quiet time."

Jesus says in this very text that only one thing is required and that one thing won't be taken away from her. In fact, the offer seems to be for Martha to join Mary in this one thing. *Come on in Martha, it's time to take the many things and make it one thing.*

Churches, it's time to become a church that embraces the posture of Mary. There are far too many anxiously driven churches and not nearly enough sitting at the feet of Jesus. Anxious churches, like Martha, are obsessed with many things: activities, serving, attendance, giving, building projects, hype, novelty, fundraising, social media posts, vision statements, big events, etc. Non-anxious churches may have these things but they aren't the main thing nor are they even the drive behind the machine. In fact, there is no machine to drive.

Now is there anything wrong with these things listed above? Maybe or maybe not. I think there are many variables to consider and we will look at much of this throughout this book. Arguing that these things are all bad would be like arguing that cooking dinner is also bad. What Martha was doing wasn't sinning but it was certainly missing the mark of discipleship. It was doing a lot and even producing a lot, but the fruit it was producing was a temporary meal instead of an eternal meal.

Introduction

I want to be clear, I don't want to shame Martha and glorify Mary. Later in the book, we will see Martha's servant attitude as something that is to be commended. The larger goal of this book is to talk about the anxiousness that we all carry with us into leadership and into ministry, using Mary and Martha as examples of the way in which we approach Jesus and discipleship; and the manner in which we approach ministry and church leadership.

Churches that embrace the Martha posture in this text will do lots of things, have good results, and be able to point to many cool metrics, but will ultimately miss making disciples who make disciples. The churches, on the other hand, that embrace the Mary posture aren't simply lazy churches or churches that don't have ideas or go places or do things. There are many churches that simply exist, but this is not actually the posture of Mary. I can think of many churches that are currently dying near my house and their mindset isn't of Mary. It's actually probably the mindset of their brother Lazarus. They need a resurrection, for they've been in the tomb for too many days and they stinketh.

It's easy to create a false dichotomy that busy churches equate to the perspective of Martha and idle churches equal the perspective of Mary in this passage. Honestly, if that's the choice maybe it is better to be a church with Martha's approach. We could even create more false dichotomies like caring about attendance or crunching budgets is a church with Martha's disposition and churches with Mary's disposition on the other hand would simply "see what happens!" However, this is a false dichotomy too. You are looking at the outward appearances instead of the heart.

Anxious churches can be idle and non-anxious churches can be off doing something. For example, let's say there is a community that has both an anxious church and a non-anxious church. In this same community, there has been an influx of homelessness. The anxious church could be too nervous to respond to the homelessness so they do nothing and say nothing, while the non-anxious church in town takes up a sleeping bag drive.

Churches that sit at the feet of Jesus are not lazy. Laziness is not Mary's posture. Since it is the art of not caring about anything more than ease. Whole churches can take the lazy approach. However, sitting at the feet of Jesus necessitates a growth in Christlikeness and Jesus was certainly not lazy or idle. Therefore, it's not fair to look at a church and say, *Wow they never do anything, must be a non-anxious church!*

Introduction

Don't over-focus on the sitting position of Mary. While this is important, it's only an outward sign of an inward frame of the heart. Mary doesn't forever remain seated. In fact, we know from the Scriptures, she physically followed Jesus. Thus the posture was movement, a movement that is an abiding movement and not an anxious movement. This is the key.

Jesus in Luke 10 isn't saying that following him means to never plan or work but instead to do things with the proper overflow. When we sit at the feet of Jesus first we can then be empowered by him in our tasks and preparations. When we do this planning and work first, we never have the time to sit at the feet of Jesus and we lose the power to do these things with sustainability. Mary shows that what is necessary about discipleship is putting the first things first.

Following the example of Mary is actually following the example of Jesus. For not only does Jesus take this opportunity to teach discipleship to and through the example of Martha and Mary, John 5 tells us that Jesus only did what he saw the Father doing.[3] John 15 calls us to abide in Jesus as He has abided in his Father; His primary posture that of resting and abiding in his Father's love.[4]

Jesus also showed us what it looks like to lead non-anxiously. He was never in a hurry, rushing from one place to another. Even when the crowds overwhelmed him, Jesus didn't conform to their anxiety but instead continued to lead from a place of deep dependence, dependence on the Father we, ourselves, can learn through his Spirit.

Maybe I am getting ahead of myself but this is what I want to explore. How do we allow ourselves to become a non-anxious church in a church culture that glamorizes the casserole that Martha makes? This is the question I seek to answer in this book. Many pastors and churches are looking for direction right now, wondering what is the way forward when it seems like anxiousness is running amok.

Let's journey together.

---

3. John 5:19
4. John 15:10

Chapter 1

How Did We Get Here?

We have to ask a couple of very important questions, "How did we get here?" or maybe "Where did it all go wrong?" The simple answer to those questions is that it's always been this way, but westernism made it the focus. What I mean is anxiety has always been an undercurrent of human complexity and thus from the very beginning we see anxious humans. These humans created anxious communities and anxious cities with anxious systems. Westernism brought that anxiety to the forefront and found a way to market it into a billion-dollar industry.

All humans have struggled to find their way in this anxious world. Adam and Eve eating the fruit from the Tree of the Knowledge of Good and Evil, then hiding, and subsequently blaming each other are examples of anxious decisions.[1] We see murder and chaos to follow in the next generations.[2] Humans are beginning to make a world shaped by anxious decisions.

This would be the world we all would be born into, a world full of deep human insecurities followed by our own personal ways of masking it. This chronic feeling of things being not quite right within will be the channels for our pride, anger, narcissism, sexual excursions, jealousy, idolatry, envy, drunkenness, self-loathing, retreating from people, comparison, workaholism, greed, and an unhealthy drive to success.

In a casual journey through the Bible, and then through the rest of history, we see humans finding their own anxiety-coping mechanisms in

1. Genesis 3:6–8
2. Genesis 4–6

an anxious world. This is why the Bible is entirely focused on shalom and bringing shalom which we often translate as peace. However, it is better understood as wholeness, since the word peace seems to mainly indicate in our language an absence of war and a lack of violence. This could be a part of shalom, but it's not the fullness of the word. Instead, wholeness indicates this idea that things are as they should be, completely and utterly whole and at rest. Jesus is the one in whom shalom is found fully and completely and when we sit at his feet and learn his way, we not only enter into his shalom; but we begin to see it infiltrate throughout our lives, our families, and our churches.

When the Bible talks about shalom it does so on two levels. First, shalom comes through this idea of wholeness in an external way penetrating the world around us; the shalom in creation and in systems and structures. While there is a great demand biblically for this wholeness to start now, we know that ultimately it will be fulfilled completely someday. Second, shalom comes inwardly through wholeness infiltrating a person's well-being. This can start right now, this very second.[3] Jesus can bring us peace through His Holy Spirit and this showcases a fantastic Christian reality of "Christ in Us!" I would guess that both versions of shalom have a tendency to feel like pipe-dreams to some of us with our world in chaos. How can it be brought to wholeness? This seems so far away especially for many communities that are in a constant state of unrest. The second kind of shalom can also feel like a faraway dream too, for our life is chaos. How can we find wholeness when our lives are like this? Even if you wouldn't define your life as chaos, it probably still feels far-fetched to say it's in the state of shalom. This underlying inner-anxiousness that is intersecting with an anxious world is constantly infiltrating our well-being. *The world is complex and thus shalom can break down. Life is complex and thus shalom can break down.*

The Bible's response to this is, *Peace has come!*[4] God brings forth peace. That's who He is and that's what He does. From the very beginning in creation, the Scriptures say that God began to bring forth goodness out of a void. Right at the beginning of Genesis, we see these words, "Now the earth was formless and empty, darkness was over the surface of the deep, and the Spirit of God was hovering over the waters."[5] God then began to create and after the day was over he looked over his creation and declared it good.

---

3. Acts 10:36, Romans 5:1, 8:6, 15:13, Phil. 4:7
4. Luke 2:14
5. Genesis 1:2

How Did We Get Here?

The Hebrew word we translate here "*good*" is *ṭôb* which like most Hebrew words is layered with meaning and richness. It is truly best translated as *good* but it has a deeper meaning of rightness, pleasantness, harmony, things being how they should be. Thus, it's a very similar concept and thought as shalom. Shalom is often the idea of bringing wholeness while *ṭôb* is the wholeness to begin with, as things should be from the start. Goodness comes out of the overflow of the nature and character of God who is good. He brings goodness with his creation and his people through the Shalom of Jesus. In this same way, Isaiah 9:6–7 says that a Messiah will come and be called the "Prince of Peace" and the kingdom (government) He brings will be peace with no end. We need to understand that Jesus brings wholeness to us and our insecurities; individually and in His family. The church becomes the outpost of this kingdom of shalom that has no end.

When Jesus showed up as a baby, his birth is referred to in Luke 2:14 as bringing forth peace. The angels declare; "Glory to God in the highest heaven, and on earth, peace to those on whom his favor rests." Jesus then began to bring forth a ministry of shalom as he "brought good news to the poor, proclaimed freedom to prisoners, gave sight to the blind, set the oppressed free and proclaimed the year of the Lord's favor."[6]

Jesus said to us, "I have told you these things, so that in me you may have peace. In this world, you will have trouble. But take heart! I have overcome the world."[7] It's one thing to preach it, but it's an entirely separate thing to live it and lead it. The world is drawing us towards the illusion of control that in reality only brings about anxious chaos, because we simply cannot control the majority of what happens in life. In this world, we will have trouble, cause trouble, bring trouble, and step into trouble. Trouble will happen to us and trouble will happen from us. Yet, shalom is found in Jesus.

This isn't the first time He taught this concept in the Gospel of John. A couple of chapters before He spoke of the troubles in this world, he said something similar in John 14:27: " Peace I leave with you; my peace I give you. I do not give to you as the world gives. Do not let your hearts be troubled and do not be afraid." It couldn't be any more clear: *There is peace that the world tries to give you, yet it's an illusion. Then there is peace that I give and it is true peace.*

6. Luke 4:18–19
7. John 16:33

He calmed literal storms and spoke peace into them. He also spoke peace into the fear he found in his disciples.[8] We see this underlying anxiety in his disciples, the same anxiousness we find within ourselves when we are also in the midst of a storm (literal or figurative). Throughout his ministry, Jesus is bringing shalom and his followers are bringing anxiousness.

As humans, we seem prone to want control, while Jesus continues to beckon us into the adventure of dependence. He slowly teaches us that to hold tight to the wheel of life is to only bring about more anxiety and to let go is to find more wholeness. When you look at the church, the bride of Christ, do we seem to be a gathering of saints that are bringing about peace or are we exhibiting anxiety? Are we grasping for control, or demonstrating what it looks like to let go?

It's not just shalom that God brings, though that certainly feels like more than enough. The shalom that comes also carries with it a structure or an organization. Actually, neither of those words are perfect words to describe what comes with shalom, for both words carry too many negative connotations. Maybe the best word is ordering. The shalom that comes from God brings with it an ordering of life that helps nurture the shalom in our journey and in our world.

God set up a helpful way of organizing and orchestrating his people in The Book of Numbers. The people were called and gathered under his name. He's constantly shepherding his people into wholeness and shalom. You may not have realized it, but Numbers is a very helpful discipleship book. In the first four chapters, we see something amazing that most people probably miss because, let's be honest, if you don't know what you are looking for at first blush, it's boring.

In the first four chapters, we see God bringing about a census and organizing the tribes based on how they camp and how they move. I know, I know you're thinking; *Wait! I thought you said this wasn't boring. You literally could not have mentioned a more boring topic than counting people and telling people where to pitch their tents.*

Hang with me for a minute. I promise it's helpful for our journey together, because what we see is that God is establishing order. Numbers 2:1–2 says, "The Lord said to Moses and Aaron: 'The Israelites are to camp around the tent of meeting some distance from it, each of them under their standard and holding the banners of their family.'"

---

8. Mark 4:35–41

How Did We Get Here?

This is how it would be set up: the Tabernacle would be at the center of the camp (where the presence of God resides). The Levites would camp around this and then each tribe would camp in formation behind the preceding tribe. The way they arranged their camp was to be ordered in such a way that it all centered around God. They formed their camps and their lives around Him. This Israelite community was to be a community under God, around God, and centered to God, the source of power, strength, and comfort; a community that was primarily centered on being with God. It's easy to see how this historical camping throughout the wilderness becomes a powerful illustration, a paradigm for our formation as Christians. We are to center our whole life around the presence of God and arrange it accordingly.

Applying this thought to the context of this book, we are to do the same with our leadership in the church. We center all that we do around God. What I just said above about the Israelite community in Numbers is now spiritually the goal for the church. The church is to be a community under God, around God, centered in God, the source of power, strength, and comfort; a community that is primarily centered on being with God.

God has given us the means to continue ordering our lives and our churches around Him. Being a non-anxious church won't accidentally fall into place; not with everything in our world working against us. We need to carve out the space for surrender to God and dependence on Him. We need to see where we are anxious, where we lack peace, and where we need order to help us find our way back.

In a general sense, we as a church culture have seemingly lost our way towards shalom and order, forsaking that for control, programs, hype, ambition, and fame. The way to the latter is through a process of anxiety. We've redefined anxiety so it doesn't seem like or feel like it. But when I talk with pastors on the verge of burnout or quitting their ministry jobs and going back into marketplace jobs, I see exhaustion. Sometimes these exhausted pastors have thrown the baby out with the bathwater and they've lost their faith, but mostly it seems like they are exhausted with the church. If the church can produce exhaustion at a higher rate than the world, then what is the church offering that actually changes lives?

A non-anxious church will make decisions and lead in such a way that they are finding peace and the way of Jesus in their decisions. Jesus said his way was easy and his burden was light. The church as an institution sure doesn't seem to showcase that very well. It actually often feels like it presents Jesus' way as hard and heavy. Why? We've joined our own anxiety and desire for control with the ways of the western world that has taught us that success and ambition is the secret sauce to a happy life. That busyness and business are how to make disciples. We've taught that the more you do, the more you attend, the more you serve, the closer you are to Jesus. Isn't this exactly what Jesus said was Martha's problem? Has the church tried so hard to make many things the requirement when it's actually "few things, really just one thing," as Jesus said to Martha?

To get back to the question that kicked off this chapter, "How did we get here?" the answer is that we've always been here as we've seen from the beginning of creation with Adam and Eve in the Garden of Eden. We see anxiousness in his first disciples until Acts 2 when it seems that dependence on the Holy Spirit became the primary focus. We see it in the first churches. These first-generation churches were often a train-wreck of anxious leadership. The apostles worked tirelessly to help these churches prevent the ways of the world from infiltrating their midst. The letter titled 1 Corinthians is a fantastic example of how early church leadership was running amok with anxiety-producing leadership. Paul was helping iron this out in the letter.

Each generation of Christians after the apostles worked to find their own way in their new community of shalom bringers. As John Dickson so brilliantly points out in his book *Bullies and Saints,* there was always a leaning towards ambition, control, and power with a reformation to follow a few generations later; only to lean back into it all over again. Dickson mentions how even in the same generation there would be those practicing the way of Jesus and those being disruptive to the gospel in the name of Jesus.[9] This concept is no different in our current generation.

Here we are again today with a specific westernized version. Let's use the "American Dream" as an example. What is this dream? It's to "make it." And by "make it," "it" means being financially wealthy, leading a comfortable life, and maybe having a little bit of influence and power in the community. It would be owning a big house with the idea of eventually getting a bigger one, and having a nice job with the idea of eventually getting paid more. Now in this century, we've even added to this dream the ambition of having an increasing number of followers or people you influence.

How does it look to apply the American Dream to the church? Think about what we consider a "successful" church. It's what? Financially wealthy, leading a comfortable life, with maybe a little bit of influence and power in

---

9. Dickson, *Bullies and Saints,* 1–2.

its community. It's owning a big building with the idea of eventually getting a bigger one; having a sizable budget but eventually getting a bigger one; having a big congregation with eventually getting a bigger one; adding influence and more congregants to influence (for good or ill).

I had a wonderful older gentleman kindly give me advice when I first became a lead pastor. He told me that the key to being a good pastor is to care about the "ABCs": Attendance, Building, and Cash. If I could increase all three of those, I'd be doing all right. Wow! If that's what it means to be a pastor, I was called into the wrong thing. I truly believe his heart was in the right place, but he simply was nurtured and trained in this style of church culture. Yet, this style of church culture is anxious and full of an unhealthy pace.

We've all been taught that the way to be a great church is to embrace the posture of Martha in Luke 10. Jesus reminds us that the way to be a great church is to embrace the posture of Mary. There is a path forward. There is hope for cultivating shalom in your church and in your ministry, but first, we need to keep digging into the roots of the problem.

Chapter 2

Anxious Pastors

It wasn't long ago that churches were mostly shaped by the people who attended and were invested in them. The pastors who were hired often felt like the outsider coming into a pre-existing family, and worked to pastor in that context. Some denominations decided that for small churches they wouldn't even place a local pastor, but use one pastor for a number of churches in the area. There are some small towns that have this model today.

A new person coming to a community in that era would decide which church to attend primarily based on the people there and the fellowship it offered. The pastor was simply the public theologian and hired-hand to help pastor the people in that community. However, the pendulum has swung almost entirely to a pastor-focused model. Now if a new person steps into a church, they see the church as pastor-centric. They decide if they like the pastor and his preaching and they attend another church if they don't. The congregants often find it easier to leave a church if they don't like the pastor than get a new pastor. Congregations in the previous era ran out the pastor first.

Both of these models have their blatant problems and we've seen the fruit of them. The balance is somewhere in the middle, when the pastor can be the pastor and the congregants can be the congregation; each having a deep love for the other as they journey together. However, our anxiety doesn't allow this to be the case and our want of control is too strong to allow the balance to remain for very long.

Anxious Pastors

Today, pastors are almost exclusively responsible for the direction the church is headed. Their voice will dictate so much of how the church functions and where it goes. The congregants will often look like the pastor. If the pastor is vain, we will often see a very vain congregation. If the pastor votes in a particular direction the majority of the church will vote that way too.

I know these are broad generalizations but there's truth found in the broad strokes even if they aren't true in each and every context. This being said — the pastor has a lot of say in the health of a church. Typically, a church is anxious because the pastor hasn't helped it overcome this. In some cases, the pastor has only enabled and furthered the anxiousness.

We need to take a look at anxious pastors. There are really two types of anxious pastors. First, there are the pastors who create anxious congregations, and second, pastors who actually create non-anxious congregations but struggle to be a non-anxious pastor. If you are a pastor, as we journey through both types, ask yourself how you fit into these types. If you aren't a pastor, but a church leader, you can also ask similar questions. As a church leader, you have others following your example. If you are neither a pastor nor a church leader, hopefully, this chapter will allow you to understand and give grace to your pastor. I ask you not to go and slam this book on their desk and demand that they become a non-anxious pastor. Instead, pray for your pastor. I would be willing to bet they didn't jump into ministry hoping to create an anxious church or be anxious themselves. There is a lot of weight in being a pastor and there is so much working against being non-anxious.

This is the point in the book where you are probably wanting to tell me that poor Martha gets a bad rap. She isn't the villain and her intentions are pure and meaningful. She truly just wants to serve Jesus, and you would be completely right. Yet, that's exactly the point, that serving Jesus doesn't always equate to being with Jesus. Jesus isn't condemning Martha and neither does he condemn you, but he is offering a gentle rebuke to her misplaced devotion.

As we look back into the story, let's pick up on some of the wonderful intentions of Martha and where exactly things seemed to go wrong. This will also help us find our way forward in this anxious world as we long for a non-anxious church. Luke 10:38 says, "As Jesus and his disciples were on their way, he came to a village where a woman named Martha opened her home to him." Martha checks a wonderful and beautiful box for following the way of Jesus; hospitality. She "opened her home to Jesus." In fact, she is the only person recorded in the Gospels as doing this for Jesus. Now there were others who invited Jesus to their home or times when Jesus even invited himself. Martha, though, is the only one who "opened her home to Jesus." The imagery of this is fantastic, for opening ourselves and our homes to Jesus is really the biggest step in our journey with Jesus. Inviting Jesus over for a visit gives us the idea that he is welcome to come that one time. Opening our home to Jesus means he can come whenever he wants, stay as long as he wants, and truly make himself at home. This is what we are hoping for in any salvation and discipleship journey. Open your heart and life to Jesus to do with them what He wants and to make himself at home. This opening of the heart and life to Jesus is most likely how your pastor became a pastor. This is how missionaries become missionaries. This is how many sold-out Christians become completely on board with the mission of Jesus. They have opened their homes to Jesus. Their lives are completely on board with the call and mission of Jesus.

This is Martha. She is the sold-out Christian. She has her car presets tuned to the Christian radio stations. She is wearing her cross necklace. She has her name imprinted on the front of her Bible. She comes to church whenever it is open. She is a small group leader, an usher on Sunday; she sings on the worship team, and she is one of the first to sign up for that new class the church is offering. She doesn't have any skeletons in the closet. When trying to define her sins she probably would have to answer like Michael Scott from the TV show "The Office," "Why don't I tell you what my greatest weaknesses are? I work too hard. I care too much. And sometimes I can be too invested in my job."[1] She's literally the person every pastor wishes they could clone. If it weren't for Jesus' gentle rebuke in this text we would all hold her up as the prime example of what a Christian looks like.

When I graduated Bible School and became a youth pastor, the secretary in our office was named Martha, and she would say that her parents named her prophetically as she became the epitome of Martha in this text. She is an amazing lady. She grew up as a missionary kid in Africa and as an adult worked at a church. I honestly think when I get to heaven she will be handing me a bulletin at the pearly gates. She's such a natural servant with an amazing gift for hospitality. Exactly like Martha of Bethany. These Marthas love Jesus and long to serve him and truly that's how God created

---

1. The Office, "The Job."

them. Both would admit after considering Luke 10 that they have to work to sit at the feet of Jesus. However, let's not get ahead of ourselves.

Luke 10:39 says, "She had a sister called Mary, who sat at the Lord's feet listening to what he said." Since Jesus held Mary as the standard in this section of scripture and not Martha, we have forever put Mary's name first and referred to them as "Mary and Martha." I never hear anyone say, "Martha and Mary." Yet the text itself doesn't flip this order, the Bible starts out with the story being Martha's and Mary stole the show. Luke records the story of Martha explaining her as having a home that she opens to Jesus. And Martha has a sister who sits at the Lord's feet. If we stopped there, these sisters would have been iconically labeled as "Martha and Mary." Martha has a home. Martha has a sister.

Luke 10:40–42: "But Martha was distracted by all the preparations that had to be made. She came to him and asked, 'Lord, don't you care that my sister has left me to do the work by myself? Tell her to help me!' 'Martha, Martha,' the Lord answered, 'you are worried and upset about many things, but few things are needed — or indeed only one. Mary has chosen what is better, and it will not be taken away from her.' "

If you read all this but stop before you read Jesus' reply — would you at any point say that Martha is worried or anxious? You might think so because Luke tips off the direction he is going with this narrative in using the word "distracted" (as the NIV translates it). However, just doing "preparations that had to be made" seems important. It's Jesus' words that introduce us to the underlying anxiety that is coursing through Martha at this moment. I would guess that if we stopped Martha before Jesus spoke and asked her how she was feeling, she wouldn't have said anxious. I bet she would have said busy or grateful to serve or even excited that Jesus showed up.

Anxiousness has a way of hanging out behind other emotions and experiences without our realizing that it is there; possibly because we are used to it. It seems to always be there in some way which makes it hard to recognize. Jesus sees through the busyness, the excitement, the preparations and sees anxiousness. Jesus knows how to get to the root of our issues with a simple statement. If Jesus had a mic at this point, he would have dropped it.

The greek word for "worried" here is helpful in our study: "merimnao," which is used a few other times in the New Testament. Most importantly we see it in Matthew 6:25–34. Jesus uses this word a handful of times in this sermon as he preaches about worry:

> "Therefore I tell you, do not worry (merimnao) about your life, what you will eat or drink; or about your body, what you will wear. Is not life more than food, and the body more than clothes? Look at the birds of the air; they do not sow or reap or store away in barns, and yet your heavenly Father feeds them. Are you not much more valuable than they? Can any one of you by worrying (merimnao) add a single hour to your life? "And why do you worry (merimnao) about clothes? See how the flowers of the field grow. They do not labor or spin. Yet I tell you that not even Solomon in all his splendor was dressed like one of these. If that is how God clothes the grass of the field, which is here today and tomorrow is thrown into the fire, will he not much more clothe you—you of little faith? So do not worry (merimnao), saying, 'What shall we eat?' or 'What shall we drink?' or 'What shall we wear?' For the pagans run after all these things, and your heavenly Father knows that you need them. But seek first his kingdom and his righteousness, and all these things will be given to you as well. Therefore do not worry (merimnao) about tomorrow, for tomorrow will worry (merimnao) about itself. Each day has enough trouble of its own."

This is an important text when we consider the anxiety that not only was prevalent then, but is still with us today. As Jesus preaches the sermon on the mount he cautions that worry will actually decrease the years of your life. This has only recently been backed up by science in the last couple of decades.[2]

"Merimnao" is a fascinating greek word. The Greek-English Lexicon of the New Testament defines it this way: "To have an anxious concern, based on apprehension about possible danger or misfortune—to be worried about, to be anxious about."[3]

Jesus looks at Martha busy "doing." She has opened her home to Jesus but He looks beyond the production and sees merimnao in her. He sees an "anxious concern based on apprehension about possible danger or misfortune." What are you worried about, Martha? What possible danger or misfortune could you be anticipating?

We could do some guessing. Could it be that she wanted to impress Jesus? Would he approve of her and her hospitality? Is she a good enough host

---

2. Meier et. Al., *Increased Mortality Among People With Anxiety Disorders*, 216–21.
3. Louw and Nida, *Greek-English Lexicon of the New Testament*, 25.225.

for the Lord? Would he judge her meal or think her house was a bit messy? Would he see her as a heretic if she said something a little bit wrong? Would he think she wasn't wealthy enough? Maybe not poor enough? Would there be enough food? Is she thinking; *Have I done all that Jesus needs of me? Have I served Jesus adequately?* Is she worried about Mary breaking gender roles? Is she worried that Jesus will think it rude?

It probably wasn't simply one of those questions and insecurities that were bubbling up, but likely many of them. The rebuke from Jesus should be ringing in our ears right now: "many things." So many things to worry about. This is how pastors who open their homes and hearts to Jesus also find themselves in a state of merimnao. What are you worried about, pastor? What possible danger or misfortune could you be anticipating? Like Martha, many things. So many things.

- Am I a good enough pastor?
- What if the church isn't growing numerically?
- Should we always be pursuing more people?
- What if the church is struggling financially?
- How should the money be budgeted? What are the top priorities for the money?
- What about the election? Should I use my platform for helping people vote?
- What about the crazy Republicans in my church?
- What about the crazy Democrats in my church?
- How do I reach the Libertarians since they won't come to my church?
- Should we build a new building? Upgrade our building? How about a balcony?
- That church up the street seems to be doing better than us. Are we not good enough?
- What about the culture all around us? Do we run from it? Attack it? Conform to it?
- How do I build a biblical worldview into my church? Is that important?
- Should I address   topic? I saw someone on the internet telling people to leave the church "if your pastor doesn't talk about   t h i s Sunday!" Maybe I need to.

- What about my staff? What positions are most important? What ministries need to be included?
- How about the counseling appointment I just had? Seems hopeless.
- How do I lead these people?
- Who should be on which committee?
- What about my family?
- How do we market our church for young families? Older couples? Singles? Teens? Young Adults?
- What about this theological issue? Seems like a big deal.
- How about this other theological issue?
- How do I talk about _____ without being crucified by one side and praised by another when I'm simply trying to be biblical?

So many things. This is honestly the tip of the iceberg for all the questions that roll through a pastor's week. It's no wonder there are so many anxious pastors and anxious churches.

What causes pastors to find themselves being caught up in a state of merimnao and turning their anxiousness into an anxious church? The first mistake is that pastors allow themselves to be pulled in all these directions. However, that's not the only way a pastor gets caught up in a state of merimnao.

Some arrive on the scene fully ready to lead their church into an anxious future but clothe that anxiety in vision statements and building strategies. There are many pastors who won't be pulled in all these directions mentioned above. However, it doesn't make them any less anxious. These anxious pastors have a set direction and they are headed for it. This is the second way a pastor becomes an anxious pastor — through toxic ambition.

Chapter 3

Ambitious Pastors

WHEN WE WRESTLE WITH our own inner anxiousness we can often channel it in ways that the world praises. I said this in the introduction, but to reiterate the point, anxiousness can hide behind a strong work ethic and good intentions. This can clearly be the case for ambitious pastors.

As I have already mentioned, there is no way that Martha would have identified her feelings as anxious, yet that is what Jesus says they were. She may have even identified them as ambitious. Ambition is considered a good feeling while anxiousness is considered a bad feeling. Often we tell ourselves that our anxiousness is simply ambition. Think about how we have cloaked our anxiousness with a nicer word like ambition. We rationalize first but our motive may be different:

- We want to see the church succeed (in the way we define it).
- We want to see people come so they can know Jesus (increasing numbers doesn't hurt either).
- We want to see people get baptized (makes for a cool picture on Instagram).
- We want to see giving increase, of course, because we've raised up generous people (having more money gives us a feeling of security and success).

There are many more ways we have rationalized our anxiety with holy intention. And maybe your rationalizations are ways in which you are trying to regain control of your desires. Sure, a part of you wants a higher attendance, more giving, and a bigger building but it's only for holy reasons. God has called you to *build* the church, right? At best, the motives for this thinking are mixed — a little bit of the flesh mixed in with the Spirit — when the flesh gets in the way of what the Spirit wants to do. However, I have a feeling more pastors than are willing to admit are actually truly ambitious and this holy intention is simply a mask for their own personal ambition.

IS AMBITION ENTIRELY BAD?

Let's start by speaking about ambition in general terms and then we should look at pastoral ambition. Ambition is a very interesting topic. On the one hand, it's necessary and even helpful. On the other hand, it's dangerous and can kill you and others along your path. There's an unattributed quote that says, "Ambition is like water. Humans need it to live but too little will weaken and kill you. Conversely, too much and you'll drown."[1] This about sums it up. Without any ambition, you will end up lazy with no direction or motivation in life. If you think of the least ambitious people in your life you will picture a lazy person wandering aimlessly through life. This certainly isn't the goal for anyone. With too much ambition, you will end up lonely, because ambition will destroy relationships in every sphere of life if left untamed. You may, in fact, end up at the top of your position with the money, fame, cars, etc., but with no deep relationships because your ambition has pushed everyone away.

The hardest part of our westernized culture is that it has made ambition a virtue. We celebrate the great success of people and we rationalize away the cost it took them to get there. We celebrate the CEO that led his business to great success but lost his family in the process. A story like this will make a great movie someday but it's far too common. We celebrate the politician who stepped on everyone to get to the top and rationalize the cutthroat strategy it took to get there. We celebrate the company that became a huge conglomerate and pretend we didn't realize they used child labor to get there. Maybe closer to home, we celebrate the church planter who built a big church but had a moral failure. We may demonize the sin that the church planter fell into but we don't condemn the ambition that led him into a frenzy.

1. Anonymous, *Metamia*, lines 17–18.

Ambitious Pastors

We think to ourselves, *Well it won't be me, I'm not* that *ambitious. My ambition is checked!* I would encourage you to ask those closest to you if you have your ambition in check. Ambition always hurts those closest to us first. While the outside world may be celebrating your success, your friends and family are watching you slip away. Do you find yourself making excuses to work more? To check your email at any moment? What do you find yourself doing when you first wake up? If it's tackling more emails or responding to texts or jotting down more ideas for your job, it's time to re-evaluate your ambition. You may be thinking, *But my work needs me!* No, your pride needs your work. Your insecurities need to feel valued.

The way of Jesus is humility. Not bigger and faster. Not hurried and hustled. It's slower. There's a balance of work and rest.

What if you are a pastor? Is it okay for a pastor to be ambitious? I think it depends on your definition of ambition and what it entails for you and for your church. When we get into the next chapter on non-anxious pastors this will iron itself out even more. But for now, let's get that journey started with an answer to the question of ambition. According to the New Nave's Topical Bible the list of ambitious people in the Bible is as follows:

- Lucifer — Isaiah 14:12–15
- Eve — Genesis 3:5–6
- The builders of Babel — Genesis 11:4
- Aaron and Miriam — Numbers 12:2–10
- Korah and his co-conspirators — Numbers 16:3–35
- Abimelech — Judges 9:1–6
- Absalom — 2 Samuel 15:1–13, 18:18
- Ahithophel — 2 Samuel 17:23
- Adonijah — 1 Kings 1:15
- Sennacherib — 2 Kings 19:23
- Haman — Esther 5:–13, 6:6–9
- Diotrephes — 3 John 9–10[2]

---

2. Nave and Viening, *The New Nave's Topical Bible,* "Ambition."

The startling thing about this compiled list is that there is literally not one story of good ambition to be found. It's all negative. It's all considered not healthy and not holy.

To keep expanding on this idea, Jesus talks about ambition in multiple places, and as followers of his way, we need to consider his words on this topic carefully. Jesus was presented with ambition right out of the chute. Luke 4:5–8 records the story in this way, "The devil led him up to a high place and showed him in an instant all the kingdoms of the world. And he said to him, 'I will give you all their authority and splendor; it has been given to me, and I can give it to anyone I want to. If you worship me, it will all be yours.' Jesus answered, 'It is written: 'Worship the Lord your God and serve him only.'"

Martha, I will give you all the best recipes and the cleanest house and your honored guest will love you the most.

The disciples explored this topic of ambition when they argued about who was the greatest among the twelve. We see this in Mark 9:33–37, Matthew 18:1, Luke 9:46, and even more blatantly when the sons of Zebedee and their mother asked for specific seats on the right and the left of Jesus in his coming kingdom.[3] What does Jesus tell them? The greatest is actually the least; the one who serves others and humbles himself.

This doesn't mean you remove your ambition, but you check it with humility and wisdom. What is your job as a pastor? It is to shepherd people. 1 Peter 5:2–4 says, "Be shepherds of God's flock that is under your care, watching over them—not because you must, but because you are willing, as God wants you to be; not pursuing dishonest gain, but eager to serve; not lording it over those entrusted to you, but being examples to the flock. And when the Chief Shepherd appears, you will receive the crown of glory that will never fade away." Look at how ambition is directed in this passage.

- "Watching over them"
- "Eager to serve"
- "Examples to the flock"

And you get a reward — the crown of glory that will never fade away! What is 1 Peter reminding pastors of here? That the task of a pastor is ambition, but ambition for people — loving people. Not people in general as if

---

3. Mark 10:35 and Matthew 20:20

the word *people* indicates a big crowd, but instead individual humans. The person right in front of you. Each and every beating heart.

You would be hard-pressed to find a definition or even an outworking of ambition that isn't selfish in some way, shape, or form. The Christian calling is about putting the love of others above oneself and the one called to be a pastor is to be the first to do so. This makes it hard for ambition to grow alongside sanctification and the pastoral calling. Can you have ambition for the calling of God? Can you be ambitious in your love for others? You may be asking yourself these questions. This idea of ambition runs away from the traditional definition of ambition and works to redefine it. We need to ask deeper questions. Pastors, lean in here. Are you chasing ambition because you want to be seen? Heard? Belong? Do you think you'll be loved more by God or others if you only "succeed" in these ways? Does seeing the "success" of other churches stir in you jealousy or bitterness? If any or all of these hits close to home, remember the words of Jesus, "Come and find rest."[4] And "You are worried about many things but only one thing is necessary."[5]

We need to follow up with an important question in regards to our ambition: *Did God actually call you to build the church?* A startling aspect of the church over its history is the pastors' sense that they have to build the church, that it is part of their calling and even their God-given gifting. They seek to grow the church through dynamic preaching and effective systems. This has become so much a part of the thinking of pastors that the church planting movement has run into a major problem as it takes in potential church planters.

Church planting has changed things in a unique way. Some of the changes have had phenomenal results. Truly unchurched or dechurched people seem to prefer a church plant to a traditional church. But some of the changes have wrecked ministry and ministers. There are many pastors who have chosen the church planting route seemingly because they don't have to walk into a system that was created by someone else or for someone else. They can plant a church that is entirely their own DNA, with the models of ministry, the programs, and the style of church they want to exist. They simply want to build the church their own way.

There are so many dangers to this thinking that we don't have time in this book to break it all down. It's dangerous for the pastor, the church,

---

4. Matthew 11:28
5. Luke 10:41–42

and the overall church culture trending towards consumerism and entrepreneurship. The danger comes back to the thinking that "I am called to build the church." And since many established churches won't really let a new pastor build a church, it only makes sense to start a brand new church, one in which you can truly do what you were called to do. Build the church.

Are you actually called to build the church? The Bible only talks specifically about building the church in one passage. Matthew 16:13–18 says:

> When Jesus came to the region of Caesarea Philippi, he asked his disciples, "Who do people say the Son of Man is?" They replied, "Some say John the Baptist; others say Elijah; and still others, Jeremiah or one of the prophets." "But what about you?" he asked. "Who do you say I am?" Simon Peter answered, "You are the Messiah, the Son of the living God." Jesus replied, "Blessed are you, Simon son of Jonah, for this was not revealed to you by flesh and blood, but by my Father in heaven. And I tell you that you are Peter, and on this rock I will build my church, and the gates of Hades will not overcome it."

Jesus says, "On this rock I will build my church." Who will? Jesus will. Sure, scholars debate, and even churches split over what Jesus meant by "rock" here. For our discussion, it doesn't matter. The rock is only what he builds upon, not the builder itself. The builder? Jesus. It's always Jesus and it always will be Jesus. The pastor doesn't build the church, the leaders don't either. Neither does the denomination or preaching style or whatever. It's always Jesus.

Paul actually tells us this when he writes, "My brothers and sisters, some from Chloe's household have informed me that there are quarrels among you. What I mean is this: One of you says, 'I follow Paul'; another, 'I follow Apollos'; another, 'I follow Cephas'; still another, 'I follow Christ.' Is Christ divided? Was Paul crucified for you? Were you baptized in the name of Paul?"[6]

God may have used the gifting of Apollos and Cephas and Paul to help build the church and baptize the people, as Paul will explain as he goes on, but it's only Jesus who accomplished anything that matters — anything of major importance. Jesus was crucified and Jesus is the one in whom we are baptized. Christ isn't divided because of our church builders, since it's Jesus who builds the church.

---

6. 1 Corinthians 1:11–13

I am a pastor at a church that is 133 years old. How fantastic is it to think that this church existed long before me and, God-willing, long after me? There is no single pastor we can point to when we consider where we are today. There is no single program, building, or ministry, etc. There is only Christ. This church almost closed down a few times and this church exploded in growth a few times and yet through it all, the constant is Jesus. Amen.

Here's what you need to understand, anxious pastor: Most churches predate you and will outlive you. Thanks be to God. And if the church doesn't predate you, say you are a church planter, your aim should be that it outlives you and doesn't depend on you.

We are ready to ask this vital question: *Whose church is it really?* This question may seem obvious to answer but our lived reality is often so different from our expressed reality. This is very apparent when we ask the above question. When pastors think of the church they've been called to shepherd, they subconsciously may begin to buy into a destructive lie that the church is "their church." I hope this strikes a nerve as we unravel the primary issue at the core of anxiety and anxious people: control. We've talked about the pastor being pulled in many directions, or seeking toxic ambition, so let's now ponder the third and final way a pastor becomes an anxious pastor, and probably the most prevalent is through the struggle for control.

We all live under an illusion of control. However, it only takes one dramatic thing to happen in life for you to realize that you don't actually possess all that much control over what occurs. Think about a few examples of when we realize how little control we have over life:

- The midnight trip to the E.R.
- When we find that lump under our skin.
- When COVID-19 shut down the world.
- When you are unexpectedly fired.
- Death of a loved one.
- The drunk driver runs a stoplight.

The list could go on and on. We aren't in control, and honestly, that's truly a gift. God has blessed us by not actually giving us control over everything. It's the illusion of control that causes anxiety. What keeps us up at night and drives us to keep replaying conversations in our head or rehearsing future conversations? It is desiring control.

One of the most helpful postures for a Christian and more so for a pastor is the attitude of "It's Not Mine." God declares in Psalm 50:11: "For the world is mine, and all that is in it." The word "all" is all-encompassing in this passage. Every part of His creation actually belongs to him and he holds it all together.[7] Creation then is to do what? Declare the glory of God[8] and be good stewards of what he has put in front of us.

When the Bible speaks of humans it never mentions them as owners of God's creation, but purely as stewards. *What is a steward?* you may ask. Eerdmans Bible Dictionary defines a steward as "One designated by a master to oversee family, household, or state matters."[9] We see a great example of a steward in Genesis 43:19–25:

> "So they went up to Joseph's steward and spoke to him at the entrance to the house. 'We beg your pardon, our lord,' they said, 'we came down here the first time to buy food. But at the place where we stopped for the night we opened our sacks and each of us found his silver—the exact weight—in the mouth of his sack. So we have brought it back with us. We have also brought additional silver with us to buy food. We don't know who put our silver in our sacks.' 'It's all right,' he said. 'Don't be afraid. Your God, the God of your father, has given you treasure in your sacks; I received your silver.' Then he brought Simeon out to them. The steward took the men into Joseph's house, gave them water to wash their feet and provided fodder for their donkeys. They prepared their gifts for Joseph's arrival at noon, because they had heard that they were to eat there."

Again in Genesis 44:1: "Now Joseph gave these instructions to the steward of his house: 'Fill the men's sacks with as much food as they can carry, and put each man's silver in the mouth of his sack.'" The steward of Joseph's household was entrusted to carry out the words and instructions of his master, Joseph, using the gifting, responsibilities, and authority he had been given. This is the posture of a Christian. We are to be a good steward of all that God has entrusted to us and put before us. A good steward needs to have two very important attitudes: First, "It's not mine," and second, "I'll do my best with what's been entrusted to me."

---

7. Colossians 1:17
8. Psalm 19
9. Gossai, *Steward*, 1252.

IT'S NOT MINE

A good steward understands that all that they have has been entrusted to them. Nothing of any value is truly theirs. Think of all that you own and those things you would attach the word "my" in front of.

- My Church
- My Money
- My Kids
- My Time
- My Problems
- My Friends
- My House
- And on and on the list goes.

A lot of our anxieties come from an attitude of claiming as our own what is not ours, instead of being thankful to God for what we have. We mismanage money because we think money is for ourselves and making ourselves happy. We mismanage our kids because we believe our kids ought to be happy all the time. We mismanage our time because we believe our time is for ourselves and for making us happy. We mismanage our burdens and problems because we believe we have to get ourselves out from under them; we are *strong*! We mismanage churches because we believe the church is for ourselves and for making us happy. We need to embrace the reality that "It's not mine." The sooner we realize that God has charged us to be good stewards the sooner we can embrace our second attitude.

I'LL DO MY BEST WITH WHAT'S BEEN ENTRUSTED TO ME

If nothing is mine then why should I even care? This may be the most logical next question and this shows how much the "mine" thinking has affected us; because *why would I want to care for something that doesn't benefit* me? Yet, a good steward is responsible for much and entrusted with much. Being a steward of what God has entrusted to us doesn't mean we don't do anything. It doesn't mean we don't try or work or train or prepare, etc.

Good stewards understand that all they have been given needs to be managed to the best of their abilities.

Every so often my wife and I find ourselves dog sitting. Recently, we were watching someone's dog and we knew this dog was prone to run away. We were very cautious, making sure the front door was never left open for the dog to escape. In a moment of absent-mindedness I had a friend drop by and I spent a few minutes talking to him on the porch, when the dog snuck by me and ran into the front yard. My friend and I both turned and immediately began to chase him. The dog, we came to find out, wasn't interested in being caught but was interested in being chased. I dove, the dog ducked. I ran this way. The dog ran that way. All the while, he had a stupid grin on his face as it watched my friend and me muddy ourselves in the front yard.

The question becomes, why were we chasing this dog? It wasn't my dog. Who cares if it runs away and never comes back. The question is silly because we were to be good stewards of the dog. He was entrusted to our care in good faith because of this we couldn't let him simply run away. After this dog had a good time making fun of us trying to catch him, my wife simply called the dog in and it immediately responded. My friend and I looked at each other flabbergasted.

If we begin to understand that what is "not mine" is still entrusted to us, it gives us a reason for taking good care of whatever we have been given custody of. It may not be yours but God has temporarily allotted it to you. He's given you the ability to steward all of these things: your gifts, your kids, your money, your time, your church, etc. Think of the parable Jesus tells us about the kingdom of God in Matthew 25:14–30.

> "Again, it will be like a man going on a journey, who called his servants and entrusted his wealth to them. To one he gave five bags of gold, to another two bags, and to another one bag, each according to his ability. Then he went on his journey. The man who had received five bags of gold went at once and put his money to work and gained five bags more. So also, the one with two bags of gold gained two more. But the man who had received one bag went off, dug a hole in the ground and hid his master's money.
>
> "After a long time the master of those servants returned and settled accounts with them. The man who had received five bags of gold brought the other five. 'Master,' he said, 'you entrusted me with five bags of gold. See, I have gained five more.'

"His master replied, 'Well done, good and faithful servant! You have been faithful with a few things; I will put you in charge of many things. Come and share your master's happiness!'

"The man with two bags of gold also came. 'Master,' he said, 'you entrusted me with two bags of gold; see, I have gained two more.' His master replied, 'Well done, good and faithful servant! You have been faithful with a few things; I will put you in charge of many things. Come and share your master's happiness!'

"Then the man who had received one bag of gold came. 'Master,' he said, 'I knew that you are a hard man, harvesting where you have not sown and gathering where you have not scattered seed. So I was afraid and went out and hid your gold in the ground. See, here is what belongs to you.'

"His master replied, 'You wicked, lazy servant! So you knew that I harvest where I have not sown and gather where I have not scattered seed? Well then, you should have put my money on deposit with the bankers, so that when I returned I would have received it back with interest. So take the bag of gold from him and give it to the one who has ten bags. For whoever has will be given more, and they will have an abundance. Whoever does not have, even what they have will be taken from them. And throw that worthless servant outside, into the darkness, where there will be weeping and gnashing of teeth.'"

Before we dig into this too deeply there is a major ground rule for understanding this parable. This is about the kingdom of God as most parables are and therefore we can't understand this parable as some sort of earned righteousness. This parable is not promoting works-based Christianity. It's not even about general stewardship, but about the larger picture of stewardship; stewardship in the kingdom as we anticipate the coming of Jesus. This isn't a financial parable. Sure, Jesus cares about how you use your finances but the primary purpose of this parable is about stewardship in the Kingdom of God.

The kingdom of God has been entrusted to you — what are you going to do with it? Spread it? Go out and increase it? Bring more to God before he returns? Hide it? How we live our lives with Christ in us matters immensely. Jesus is very concerned with our stewardship in all aspects of life, since once we unite our lives with Christ, we are always in the kingdom of God. We are stewards, not owners; from the *little things* to the *big things*. We are entrusted with much so let's be faithful with much. The good news is we don't do it alone. We don't even do it in our own strength. God knows that in our own strength we can't be faithful stewards, so he left us his Holy Spirit that lives within us.

Now to get back to the larger point. Anxious pastors get duped into this illusion of control. That it is "my" church and that the success or failure completely depends on me and what I do and how I do it. Mostly, we need to get out of the way and understand we are simply good stewards of the church that God has called us to pastor.

Finally, an anxious pastor becomes so through embracing a "savior complex." This is similar to ambition and control. Yet, it's different in a unique way. Ambition isn't other-focused unless necessary, and control isn't always concerned with helping. The "savior complex" is believing that you and you alone are responsible and capable of saving someone. It can be a difficult concept for a pastor to *not* embrace, because a pastor is called to help as a major component of their job. There are so many ways a pastor helps and let me tell you, it feels good to help. Who doesn't love to feel needed? Thus, we help and then we feel good; so we want to help more and feel good more. Then we seek out even more ways to help and feel good and come to believe we are the *only ones who can help*.

Many pastors come pre-equipped with this thinking before they step into their new position, because the pastoral profession has a tendency to draw helpers and compassion warriors out of the pews and into the ministry. God has designed us to help and wants us to help others. The problem becomes when we begin to think *our* helping is the *only* helping, and when we begin to give ourselves credit and pat ourselves on the back.

There is only one Savior. That savior is not you. That savior is not me. That Savior is Jesus of Nazareth who can and will work through you, but not for your glory but for his.

We have explored all the different ways pastors can become anxious in the last two chapters but it might be helpful to close this chapter by classifying anxious pastors into two categories by how they affect their congregations. We need a deeper awareness of these two types as we move into the chapters on the larger body.

TYPE 1 — PASTORS CREATING ANXIOUS CONGREGATIONS

Anxious pastors have a tendency to draw other anxious people to them. Everyone is on board all the time. Service is the number one gift and if you aren't helping the cause you are hurting the cause. You need to be volunteering, leading, influencing, empowering, and doing. Wow, I got exhausted just writing that sentence, so imagine how exhausted the people in those congregations must be! In these churches, the way to the throne room is through the kitchen, and while you are there, please lend a helping hand. The meal and the prep isn't going to happen on its own. Pastors who are anxious put people around them who further the mission, vision, and exhaustion of the church.

TYPE 2 — PASTORS CREATING NON-ANXIOUS CHURCHES BUT WHO ARE STILL ANXIOUS

There are some anxious pastors who have the ability to lead people into the living room, set them down before Jesus and then hurry off to do their "job." In fact, they truly believe their role is to make sure they do the work of the Lord so the others don't have to. They are the hired hand and so they need to act as such. However, these relationships don't usually last long. Typically, the pastor and the church decide "it's just not a good fit," and they close the door on that chapter. The pastor is discouraged because the rest of the church isn't helping, and the church is concerned their pastor is teetering on burnout. Both would be right, but instead of finding a way towards a non-anxious church, they part ways.

I had a youth pastor friend once who left his youth pastor job at one church because he said, "No matter what I do, the kids just don't seem to care. I gave out free iPads at one event and you know what they told me? They told me they already had an iPad. I can't believe it. There's nothing I can do for them."

When we set attendance and excitement as the primary motivators for an event or gathering, we will be frustrated when there is neither attendance nor excitement. However, I think the problem was not that the kids didn't need an iPad. They needed something so much more meaningful and lasting than an iPad. They needed a non-anxious youth ministry, one to which they could come and abide in Jesus. One that would call them out of the anxiousness of the world that surrounds them, attacking them on their devices, invading their peer groups at school, and even infiltrating their homes. Jesus has given pastors and churches the vehicle (The Holy Spirit) to His kingdom but oftentimes we try to navigate in God's kingdom peddling our own bike, and we wonder why we are exhausted.

Chapter 4

Anxious Churches Fueled By Performance

"Be careful what position you accept for not every church is a safe church. There are many churches that will chew you up and spit you out." This was the advice my dad, a pastor, gave me, his son, as I was searching for a new ministry job. God was leading me out of one church and on towards another and my father was concerned I would end up at one of *those* churches.

What are *those* churches? Anxious churches. Churches that are so concerned with power, prestige, status, numbers, influence, giving, or simply entrenched in their own way of doing things that any outsider is going to ruin it for them.

How do groups of people called to the way of Jesus, reading the Bible every week, and singing songs of praise in service, become some of the ugliest groups of people in our world? The Sunday service where God gets the glory should look nothing like a business meeting where Mammon seems to get the glory, or some other destructive focus. There are countless stories of church business meetings being a place of torment and destruction; violence done in the name of Jesus and destruction carried out for the sake of the church.

How do churches get this way? It starts with a little anxiety or in some cases *a lot* of anxiety. Whether it's from the pastor or groups of influencers, the culture begins to shift to a culture of anxiousness.

Anxious Churches Fueled By Performance

Scot McKnight and Laura Barringer write about this very topic in their book *A Church Called Tov*, where they explain church culture this way: "Like any organization, every church is a distinct culture, formed and nurtured and perpetuated by the ongoing interaction of leaders and congregants."[1] They go on to say that the negative or what they call "toxic" church culture "will take root in a church's culture when the congregation and leaders interact in toxic and dysfunctional ways . . . When a church's culture becomes toxic, the challenge to resist becomes harder and harder."[2]

We need to look at these cultures as we understand the underlying anxiety that leads to the toxicity of these anxious churches. Let's return to Luke 10 and look at what Martha says; "Lord, don't you care that my sister has left me to do the work by myself? Tell her to help me!"[3]

Anxious churches are convinced they are left to do the work by themselves, and this is important for us on two fronts. First, we see that Martha is convinced the work is to be accomplished by everyone but Jesus here — it may be *for* Jesus but it is certainly not Jesus' task. There are tasks to perform for Jesus and things to do for Jesus and missions to accomplish because of Jesus. However, anxious churches miss out on doing things *with* Jesus.

Secondly, we see that Martha is convinced she has the right approach to hosting Jesus and is fearful of doing that "right approach" in a wrong way. There is too much to accomplish alone and so we need Jesus to tell Mary to help out. "Don't you care?!" My church is doing so much for your kingdom, we are the only ones that seem to be doing it the right way, and so you need to tell others to do it just like us.

I would assume many church conferences were started in this way. Many "how-to" books for churches were written in this way—this idea that "the way we do church would be helpful for everyone else if they would just do what we are doing! I hope Jesus sends more people into our way of doing church." They are looking for more cooks in the kitchen to perform for Jesus. Consequently, when we look at anxious churches we can see that they are functioning in two primary mindsets: performance and fear. In this chapter, we will look at how anxious churches function on performance, and in the next chapter, we will look at anxious churches fueled by fear.

At the beginning of Luke 10:40, we see that "Martha was distracted by all the preparations that had to be made." These preparations weren't for no

---

1. Barringer and McKnight, *A Church Called Tov*, 14.
2. Barringer and McKnight, *A Church Called Tov*, 16–17.
3. Luke 10:40

reason. She was preparing for the hosting of Jesus, presumably a big meal. Jesus was there to be waited on and served, to be shown how great a host Martha was, and how wonderful her cooking was. I've heard many pastors speak about their church services in the same way. Sunday is a "weekly Super Bowl" in which we need to have everything just right because that is when Jesus and his followers (and hopefully a few non-Christians) come to the big meal. They will say, "We prepare and practice all week for this Super Bowl!" And the reality is, the performance, when prepared rightly and cooked with the premium ingredients and perfect timing, is amazing. We love a big feast and a well-prepared table. We love being able to come and consume and then not have to do any of the work of cleanup.

The disturbing part about anxious churches is that when things are kicking into high gear and going really well, it's hard to notice the anxiety because the results are awesome. The feast is fantastic. In fact, if Jesus hadn't said anything about Martha's anxiety, the underlying anxiety would be a non-event and the well-hosted feast would take center stage. Jesus could have easily sent Mary off with Martha to help, and the story would have culminated with what great hostesses Martha (and Mary) were. The anxiety would have never been called out and would have never been noticed.

I would assume that most churches that are firing on all cylinders and performing well, would scoff at the reality that they are anxious churches. "How can you be an anxiety-laced church with results like these?!" It won't be until the wheels come off the performance, or the frantic backstage is revealed that they realize how much anxiety went into the production of the "church" every week.

When the only things left are the dishes in the sink, the mud on the carpet, and the food scraps on the floor, they will realize how exhausted they actually are. Anyone who has ever hosted an amazing party at their house doesn't realize they are exhausted until everyone leaves, and then there is still all the cleanup to take place. My wife is an amazing hostess and she loves to have people over to our house for dinners and gatherings. We've had baby showers, gender reveals, birthday parties, and even bridal showers at our house. And let me tell you first hand, there is excitement in the preparation and there is adrenaline in the party itself, but there is only exhaustion left when the party ends.

This isn't how the kingdom of God is supposed to look: exhaustion after church. Jesus said that his way was restful and easy. Certainly, the way of the performance isn't a restful or easy way. It's exhausting, and yet it's what we have labeled as a "successful church."

A church's focus on performance could stem from three different motives and we need to identify all of them if we expect to grow out of them into the restful and easy way of Jesus. Let's explore each of these three motives starting with the most unhealthy and working towards the healthiest, but still anxious way of Martha.

FOCUS ON PERFORMANCE TO BENEFIT THEMSELVES

Due to deep insecurities and inner anxieties about ourselves, there is something in us that wants to put on a show so people think of us as better than we are. This is a very common human problem. In its most basic form, it is a survival instinct, but at the most extreme it dives into narcissism. Chuck DeGroat covers this topic very well in his excellent book, *When Narcissism Comes to Church*. He says, "Narcissists do not feel like the world is safe. They might not say it out loud, but this is their inner experience. While we all use self-protective strategies, the shadow dance of a narcissist is a dance of radical avoidance of anything that threatens his grandiosity, his control, his certainty. And while the narcissist lives self-defensively, threatened by any who might be a rival or postured to stay in the one-up position in every relationship, he is really most threatened by what is hidden within. At his core, he is a scared little boy. And yet he appears angry and controlling when the repression of the shame and rage within unwittingly reveals itself, turned on others and a world he is threatened by."[4]

While we are focusing specifically on the church as a whole and not one specific person, the people in the culture dictate how the culture works. And if a narcissist or even simply an insecure but highly ambitious person is driving the culture forward, we will see a performance-driven model that benefits themselves. This model makes them feel better by pretending to be better, a "shadow dance" as DeGroat called it.[5] The church as a group of people is sucked into this way and excited by the show. It truly is cool to be part of a movement that looks great on the outside and that has fun things happening every week. The worship is big. The pastor's sermons are engaging and at times even flashy. The welcoming feeling of the church is great and the free coffee is amazing. Yet it's all a show because behind the

---

4. DeGroat, *When Narcissism Comes to Church*, 88.
5. DeGroat, *When Narcissism Comes to Church*, 87–88.

scenes, the depth and richness of their time sitting at the feet of Jesus is non-existent. The performance is for their own benefit. They want to look good so they feel good, but their own inner angst is always looming and so eventually the problems will come to the surface. Jesus actually tells us to watch out for this type of worship. In Matthew 6, right before he teaches his disciples how to pray he admonishes them in verses 1–6:

> "Be careful not to practice your righteousness in front of others to be seen by them. If you do, you will have no reward from your Father in heaven. So when you give to the needy, do not announce it with trumpets, as the hypocrites do in the synagogues and on the streets, to be honored by others. Truly I tell you, they have received their reward in full. But when you give to the needy, do not let your left hand know what your right hand is doing, so that your giving may be in secret. Then your Father, who sees what is done in secret, will reward you. And when you pray, do not be like the hypocrites, for they love to pray standing in the synagogues and on the street corners to be seen by others. Truly I tell you, they have received their reward in full. But when you pray, go into your room, close the door and pray to your Father, who is unseen. Then your Father, who sees what is done in secret, will reward you."

Notice it's not the practicing of righteousness or the giving or the praying that's the problem. It's the doing it for the performance. If, before we do something righteous, we plan for others to see it, is it really righteous? When we go to give money to a charity do we discreetly drop a social media post about it? When we pray do we make sure it has the right vibrato and excitement so people see how passionate we are? To bring it back to anxious churches—do we plan outreach events so people know that "our church was there!"? Do we give extra money to missions and make sure that our denomination is aware we did that? Do we plan a worship night so people know how amazing we are at worship?

Jesus compared this type of religion to white-washed tombs or dirty cups, looking good on the outside but on the inside full of death and dirt. "On the outside you appear to people as righteous but on the inside you are full of hypocrisy and wickedness,"[6] Jesus said using harsh words to communicate a very important point. If you are a church that focuses on performance for your own sake then you are selfish-minded and not walking in his way.

---

6. Matthew 23:25–28

FOCUS ON PERFORMANCE FOR THE BENEFIT OF THE SEEKER

The second type and probably the most prevalent type of performance-based motives we see in the church is for the benefit of the seeker. The seeker-sensitive model has become so widespread in our culture. It was made popular in the 1990s and hasn't slowed down at all in the last 30 years; it's only morphed and grown.

The goal was to put on a performance that would wow the unbeliever and have them begin attending church and eventually become a Christian. It was Christianity made cool and it worked. It's hard to call out this Martha-driven performance model. Typically it works and often it works well, especially when we are measuring things by outward appearance. It's the inner-anxiety that isn't addressed and never dealt with which causes the long-term problems. Jesus wasn't going to let Martha by with a free pass on this; *it's time to deal with the underlying issues.* "You are worried and anxious about many things."[7] *And your desire to perform is part of the covering up of this anxiety.*

Reaching the seeker is a good thing, right? Helping them find pathways into the church is what every church should be seeking, right? We are to be a lamp upon a lamp-stand and a city on a hill. This can truly be a selfless mode of church expression. Martha tries to put on the best performance for someone else, not for herself and churches can embrace the same attitude. They want to help many people come and experience the new life in Christ. This is all good and great and part of what God has called churches to. However, when we put the focus on performance we unintentionally introduce expectations that won't disciple people in the way of Jesus, but may eventually turn them off to it all completely (if not redirected).

The focus on performance teaches the roles of consumption on the part of the visiting attendees and cleanup on the part of the contributing members. To go back to the story of the dinner party; the goal of a dinner party is that our guests come and consume, enjoy themselves, and walk away pleased. When we build a church model this way we get the seekers to come, consume, enjoy themselves, and walk away pleased. None of these activities help someone walk the way of Jesus. If anything, they are counterproductive to his way. We have to re-disciple a consumer Christian

---

7. Luke 10:41

to understand the gospel isn't actually tied to advertising and product promotion. I would even argue that the biggest frustration for many pastors is that they have a church full of consumers and yet it's the model on which we are told to build.

The church that Jesus builds isn't a church about coming and consuming. It's a family. The dinner party is great to bring in people that don't belong to your family, but they always leave and are never really part of the family. They only signed up for the family newsletter and the next few big events. They'll come for the next meal but nothing more because they aren't part of the family.

It would be weird for a guest at your dinner party to assume that because they came to your get-together they can now be part of your family, and yet somehow that's what we believe about our church services. Consumption doesn't welcome people in the family. It only furthers the desire for your family to put on more consumption-related events. And for the rare few that do get pulled out of this mode and into the family, this model then teaches them that their role in the whole thing is prep and cleanup.

Think about the opportunities when churches are always pushing for people to "be involved" and "to serve." They need help with:

- Kids' ministry volunteers
- Ushers
- Greeters
- Parking lot attendants
- Bus drivers

There are, of course, many other spots someone can serve but most often we enlist a consumer into a volunteer job and the volunteer ministry is simply another opportunity for them to set the table for the dinner party and wash the dishes afterward. You say, "Well it needs to be done!" And you would be right, if you keep hosting dinner parties. Those dishes aren't going to clean themselves and that food isn't going to cook itself. And the anxious church wheel keeps on turning.

This isn't to say a church doesn't need the above volunteers, but I'm using those examples to demonstrate how the system perpetuates itself. If the goal is the Sunday service and the performance we need to put on, the major way a person can be part of the family is by serving at the Sunday service. It's similar to the dinner party at your house. If your family's main existence and purpose were these dinner parties, then the main way you can be part of that family is by preparing for them and cleaning up after them only to do it again the next week.

The church of hype, novelty, and "WOOOO!" may be great at seeing people come in the room but it does a terrible job of helping them realize that Jesus wants them in the family.

FOCUS ON PERFORMANCE FOR THE BENEFIT OF JESUS

Finally, we get to the most noble of all of the performance-driven focuses, and that is the focus on the performance for the benefit of Jesus. I truly believe that this was Martha's goal. She was preparing and cleaning, not for herself, or for a seeker, but for Jesus. She wanted him to know how much she loved him and how much she cared by what she could do for him.

It's truly a beautiful and even inspiring thing to be able to plan church services that give God all the glory. In fact, I would say that's necessary in being a non-anxious church. However, where it begins to break down is when we are preparing and performing in the hopes to impress Jesus. We want him to be pleased with us by what we can do for him. It's even a pendulum swing from the previous focus. We don't want to create consumer Christians; we instead want to create servant Christians, ones that do everything for God. In this scenario, we are on the stage and God is the only one in the audience. We are performing and God is hopefully clapping.

Skye Jethani breaks down this mindset in his book *With* as living the life in Christ "for God." He says, "The response to fat, lethargic Christians is usually a rigorous exercise routine. Ministries use many different devices to motivate people to serve, engage, and give; but their goal is the same—to transform their members from a posture of living *from* God to a posture of living *for* him"[8] (emphasis the author's). However, while this posture has a different focus it has the same result: exhaustion and frustration. We do all the work and Jesus just idly watches us perform.

People in this system become exhausted and end up burning out and/or leaving the church completely. The pastor kid stereotype works because what a pastor kid learns most from their parents is anxiety about the church. They never truly feel part of the family of God because even their own family is joined to the servitude of the performance for God. And for

---

8. Jethani, *With*, 83.

a pastor's kid, there are far more pleasurable places to experience chronic anxiety than a church. So why would we stay in church?

Martha didn't ask Jesus to come help. She didn't even consider that option because he was the guest of honor in the house. You don't ask the guest of honor to be part of the serving. Her sister, however, certainly should be helping.

Jesus sees Martha's heart of service as a heart of anxiousness and performance. He doesn't want the performance; he wants the person. He doesn't want to be a guest at the dinner party. He doesn't really want the party at all. He wants to show up to your house as it is, without you even cleaning ahead of time. He loves you for who you are, not who you want him to see. What he loved about Mary's response was the fact that she wanted to do life *with* him not *for* him. Jesus desires our presence not our airs.

In Winn Collier's biography of Eugene Peterson, he tells the story of the first time, after many years of being a pastor, that Eugene and his wife Jan needed to attend a church as a congregant. Eugene was worried that they wouldn't even be able to find a non-anxious church. "For the first time in their lives, Eugene and Jan needed to find a church. They visited a small parish close to their apartment (always his recommended way to find a church: whatever was in your neighborhood). '50 or 60 people at most, spare surroundings—simple. That's all I want in worship: a place and time to attend to God, and no pastor or priest getting in the way. Will we be able to find that?'"[9] When Eugene speaks of attending to God, it is not attending as a waiter or a servant, but as a friend; being able to sit with God and enjoy his presence. The posture of Mary of Bethany.

At this point, we need to address the reality that it's not bad to do things for Jesus. In fact, Mary of Bethany anoints Jesus with nard in John 12 for his upcoming death. We need to know that our desire to do things *for* Jesus should be to further the relationship *with* Jesus. Church Historian and Author of the book *Santa Biblia*, Justo Gonzalez, hits on this when he says, "We read the Bible, not primarily to find out what we are to do, but to find out who we are and who we are to be."[10] This *who we are* will then determine what we do, but if we work backward we are lost in production and legalism instead of relationship.

Think of it like any other relationship. Do I do things for my wife so I can forever live in the position of always doing things for my wife? That

---

9. Collier, *A Burning In My Bones*, 224.
10. Gonzalez, *Santa Biblia*, 115

would be an exhausting way to be married. I do things for my wife and she does things for me because it betters our lives with each other. When we do things for Jesus it's for the goal of being closer with him.

There are, of course, other reasons that churches might perform; for example, competing with other churches nearby, for their denomination, or even their local communities. However, the above points could be considered for these approaches too. Ultimately, they all get us back to performing for something or someone instead of finding our desire to abide in Jesus and his way.

The way forward is to no longer be fueled by a performance-driven model. It's life-sucking for the performers and the congregation. Don't be discouraged. There is hope ahead and it is attainable, but it comes with surrender. However, we need to address one more false fuel we use to run our churches.

Chapter 5

Anxious Churches Fueled by Fear

FEAR IS A POWERFUL motivator. It leads us to make all sorts of anxious decisions and manipulative choices. Many of the most destructive examples of churches and pastors that we've seen make the news in the last decade have to do with anxious churches fueled by fear. We have seen pastors use authoritarian tactics akin to a dictator, and churches so scared to ruin their precious image that they hide abuse; we should be grieved by this reality. At the root is an anxious church that has allowed their anxiousness to manifest itself into a fear-driven model.

There are two ways anxious churches are fueled by fear. First, there is the "fear of"; which is defined by making decisions and leading because the church is fearful of the results. Second, there is "fear over"; characterized by using fear to keep people in line with their way, making decisions, and leading in a corresponding manner. The former is the timid approach to leadership and the latter is the aggressive approach; both styles are fear-driven in anxious churches.

FEAR OF

I have a friend who I would call a non-anxious pastor. He works hard for the good of the people in his church. He loves them all with a steady and pastoral presence, not caught up in the anxiety of the church. However, the church he pastors has been historically an anxious church. I ask him all the time why he puts up with all their mess and he responds that it's because he was called there and Jesus still loves them.

Leading an anxious congregation towards a non-anxious future is long and hard work. (We will get to this in a later chapter as I believe it's also very important work.)

My friend once found out about a prominent volunteer leader who was sexually harassing women. He was astounded by this reality but immediately went about the work of truth-seeking, removing the leader, and helping those who had been harassed. The pushback he got from his church was not because they thought the man was innocent, but more because of the fear of walking the hard path of accountability. They were stressed about the ramifications of how the church would look, how the leader and the people who supported him would react, and how much time it would take to wade through it all. Mostly, they were fearful of this volunteer leader, his intimidation and repudiation.

My non-anxious friend was once again astounded at the audacity of the congregation not wanting to do the right thing for fear that the right thing would be too messy and hard. Eventually, my friend resigned from his position after his life was threatened by the sexual harasser and the church was still too fearful of all the ramifications to pick sides. He remained unsupported even after ending up in court trying to get a restraining order so he could protect himself and his family. The church was still fearful of the perpetrator and struggled to get behind their pastor. How sad and devastating for this pastor. Yet this is a prototypical approach of an anxious church operating in the "fear of" style. The fear of the "what if . . . " It manifests itself in many varieties. The includes fear of:

- Not enough giving
- Not enough people
- Culture
- Political agendas
- Hard work
- Messy work
- Making people angry
- Looking bad

And on and on the list goes. The easiest approach is to respond in the most anxious manner possible, whether that is through sweeping something under the rug or attacking it head-on. When we let fear dictate how we respond, it will never be the right response. It will always end up blowing up on everyone, hurting people in the process, and grieving the Holy Spirit.

When we let the "what if" questions drive the church forward into the future, the future will always be an anxious one, full of more fears and more unknown anxieties. Yet, the only answer we seem to have is more "what if" questions and more anxious responses to those "what if" questions.

- What if someone leaves our church?
- What if everyone leaves our church?
- What if we don't make budget?
- What if our building has a problem?
- What if our people begin to follow a false ideology?
- What if our people vote in the election differently than we want?
- What if a scandal were to break?
- What if we find an abuser in our church?

Anxious churches either take a passive approach to fear or an aggressive one, the passive approach is hopeful that it will all go away. Similar to the story above; what if we just quietly handle this instead of publicly? Churches have people sign non-disclosure agreements, quietly settle financially behind the scenes, run from the problems, hide the abuse, and cover up the scandal.

The aggressive approach tends to create strategies to attack the "what if" questions that plague them. They create programs that make sure people won't leave their church, or at least not very easily. They use strong motivators to get people to give so they can make budget. They rant and rave from the platform about the dangers of *that* political party so people in their church won't vote that way.

Both of these ways of handling the "fear of" approach are laden with anxiety and create only the illusion of control. We feel if we can control the narrative, we can continue to get the results our anxious system is supposed to produce. If our anxious system can combat this fear we can get back to being anxious in other ways. We were supposed to be in control! These unknowns are crashing all around us and we can't control our way out of them. Whether we do it passively through fear or aggressively through fear we are allowing ourselves to be very anxious churches. The problem with life viewed through the lens of fear is that there will always be:

- A new enemy
- A new cultural agenda
- A new vision or assignment
- A new problem or issue

The "fear of" approach also leads us to make anxious decisions that aren't always reactive but sometimes proactive. We hear about a new church model and for fear of missing out on the fruit it promises, we implement it right away. We hear about a new outreach in town and all the other "good" churches in town are doing it, and for fear of not looking like a "good" church we schedule it too. For fear that our people will get too active and involved in other things we strategically plan a full block of programs and activities (many congregants will encourage this). Even if fear is driving our church to do "good" things with wrong motives, we can still be a very anxious church for, once again, in life there will always be:

- A new mission/outreach
- More programs and events
- New church growth strategies

You may want to stop me right here and tell me there are truly things we should be fearful of, like cultural agendas and the latest threat to the gospel. Right? There are so many leaders and churches that are so scared of these supposed threats to the gospel. It seems like every year we are labeling something the latest "threat to the gospel." It has been my personal observation that this ideology usually comes from very strongly fundamentalist type Calvinistic churches. I could be wrong here, but if my assessment in even remotely right, this is baffling, because Calvinistic churches believe that someone who is saved can't be unsaved and somehow they are worried about threats to the gospel? The gospel takes root in our hearts and spreads out from us into the world. If we can't be unsaved once we are saved how can it be threatened?

However, even if you aren't an overly fundamentalist Calvinist it's important we also know that the gospel can't be threatened. Say it with me:

nothing can threaten the gospel. To threaten the gospel implies there's a bully that's arrived on the playground and the poor gospel is nervous it may get picked on or beat up. I believe that there are things that can distract you or even cause you to run the wrong way. And even if you were to run away from Christ and no longer believe, the gospel isn't dependent on you. It is unshakable. Yes, Jesus wants the gospel to take root in you, but whether you are in or out doesn't shake or diminish the power and authority of the gospel.

Let me be fair, I think that perhaps what they are worried about is a threat to the free dissemination of the gospel, or a perversion of the gospel by unbelievers, not that they'll lose their salvation. Fear still shouldn't dictate their approach to leading a church. Fear isn't the way forward in either of those worries. I believe they need not worry, because God works in hearts, and even in persecution the church grows, sometimes even flourishes more. Yes, the gospel is not dependent *on us*. Jesus feeds his sheep.

To get back to fear, the Bible wants you to be only fearful of one thing. God. Fear of God is what matters. And it's not the scared out of your mind sort of fear; it is a fear in the reverence of God.

FEAR OVER

Controlling others in fear.

I honestly believe that at times churches and leaders use the term "threat to the gospel" not as a *fear of* tactic but a *fear over* tactic. They know that if they make their people fearful of whatever that latest threat to the gospel is, it will keep them in line—keep them within whatever the preset doctrines they have decided is the most important for their people and their camp. In other words, it is used to control others in fear. It is used to keep people in line and stay obedient to their whims and ways. And sure, some of the things they call a threat to the gospel could actually be serious issues, but the phrase itself is used to inspire fear in their people and the ability to dig their heels in deeper in the "right doctrines."

There are so many fantastic books that have come out in the last few years that deal with this very topic and I would encourage you to read them if this one strikes a particular nerve in you. If *fear over* is the experience you have had or maybe you even help perpetuate, you need to read books like *A Church Called Tov* by Scot McKnight and Laura Barringer, *Jesus and*

John Wayne by Kristin Kobes Du Mez, *When Narcissism Comes to Church* by Chuck DeGroat, and others along this vein.

The "fear over" church is still deeply insecure about itself and still very much works out of inner anxieties they feel internally. However, what makes these churches different is that they manifest those anxieties into manipulation and control. They create hoops to jump through to be "in." They create lines around the boundaries so they know who is "in." They create excessive rules to bring about submission; *Christians don't wear that, drive that, read that, watch that, etc.* And they work hard to control their image in such a way that if they are told they are anxious or wrong in what they do, it's "an attack of the enemy."

All anxious churches are focused primarily on themselves whether they are performance or fear-driven. Ultimately, they are being selfish and self-serving. Even if they mask it with this false projection that they are being "seeker-sensitive" or "doing it *for* God," at the end of the day they are working to build their own brand and cover their own insecurities. As author and pastor, Andrew Wilson, once said, "Worry is what happens when you pray to yourself."[1] If we apply this to a church culture, the worry perpetuates even more self-focus, for our models of performance and fear drive us to make selfish and anxious decisions.

It's almost like an old Looney Tunes episode where there is a trap set for the "wasically wabbit" with arrows pointing into the box and the carrot there for the lure. But the cunning Bugs Bunny somehow tricks Elmer Fudd into going into his own box. The arrows pointing in and the bait (to boot) only end up trapping yourself into a game you can't keep up with and a game you can't win. Even if you have "success" for a season, we are learning over and over again that in our culture that this type of success comes with a big cost.

Eventually, the planting of all the performance and fear will give way to the fruit of performance and fear. When the fruit comes to ripeness, all the growth and acclaim that the great big tree was receiving will come crashing down because the fruit is poison. Jesus said it this way in Matthew 12:33–37:

> "Make a tree good and its fruit will be good, or make a tree bad and its fruit will be bad, for a tree is recognized by its fruit. You brood of vipers, how can you who are evil say anything good? For the mouth speaks what the heart is full of. A good man brings

---

1. Wilson, "Sermon: Do Not Worry."

good things out of the good stored up in him, and an evil man brings evil things out of the evil stored up in him. But I tell you that everyone will have to give account on the day of judgment for every empty word they have spoken. For by your words you will be acquitted, and by your words you will be condemned."

What does an anxious person bring forth out of their life? More to the point, what fruit does an anxious church produce? The most common is by far, exhaustion. This is the best-case scenario too, and so it's God's grace that this is the most common. Exhaustion may be damaging, but not as damaging as the other fruit produced by an anxious church culture, the other fruit we've seen littering the headlines for the last decade: abuse and corruption. And ultimately, all of these lead to the fruit of bitterness for everyone involved.

Chapter 6

Non-Anxious Pastors

I'M NOT SURE HOW it exactly happened, but one day I was accepting the job to be a youth pastor and a few short years later I was sitting anxiously in my office, dreaming and sweating about being the next lead pastor at the same church.

Unbeknownst to me, there was talk on the search team when I was being hired as the youth pastor about hiring the successor to the lead pastor. The current lead pastor was getting close to retirement and the church was looking to the future. I didn't know this during the interview process. To be fair to the team, they weren't putting all the eggs in that basket. They would have been fine with a different transition plan but they had their mind open to that idea. I thought I would forever be a youth pastor, and I think all youth pastors who are called to this ministry think this. It truly helps them stay grounded in the present. However, after a few years, I was preaching about ten-fifteen times a year and was overseeing all of the kids and youth. Eventually, I was offered an associate pastor position with much more adult ministry oversight. I would be doing a lot of teaching and preaching, which I love.

I was on the fast track to be the next lead pastor but I wasn't sure that was what God was up to, and I wasn't sure how to act or react. Eventually, the transition came when my predecessor retired, and the church brought in an interim pastor. He was to only work behind the scenes and I would do the primary preaching while the church and denomination took the next steps.

Let me tell you, I was anxious, and every day during this season I would wake up with my thoughts full and my schedule more full. I didn't know what to say or how to say it and yet they gave me a microphone every single week. It had the potential for a big mess and a possibility for this church to become a very anxious church with a very anxious pastor. Then the Associate Superintendent of our conference, Don Robinson, pulled me aside as he was helping us transition and working with the search team. He didn't say much to me but what he did say changed the trajectory of this season and changed the trajectory of my ministry. It was a simple concept but life-altering and church-changing. He said, "Mark, your role in this season is to be a non-anxious presence. God will handle the rest." I then proceeded to tell everyone that I was assigned to take a NAP (Non-Anxious Presence), which in some ways wasn't far from the truth.

The journey then began for me to figure out what it looked like to be a non-anxious pastor and I have never looked back. Yet like everyone, I still struggle with making anxious decisions and leading in an anxious way. The first step in my journey of discovery was learning that it is about the inner life. A non-anxious pastor will be discreet and won't be flashy or obvious, because the majority of the work of a non-anxious person and much more a pastor, happens on the inside. The overflow from that inner work is the non-anxious fruit. We tend to focus on what a pastor does and what a pastor looks like. There are entire books, articles, blogs, and social media accounts on the fashion styles made famous by celebrity pastors. We want to look the part and perform the way we are supposed to perform; say the words we are told to say and act the way people expect us to act. However, if we are only focused on what we look like on the outside, we go back to the white-washed tombs that Jesus talked about.

The inner life needs to be cultivated to truly walk the way of a non-anxious pastor. This is hard. There are no "three steps to being the most successful pastor." There's no manual on how to "kickstart your church by your leadership" that actually qualms the inner anxiety. There aren't many pastors who say that being a non-anxious pastor is natural and the first thing they do. The ones who do probably are mistaking laziness for non-anxious leading. We aren't talking about laziness or inactivity. That isn't non-anxious pastoring. By the end of this chapter, I'm sure even those folks will know there's more to be done to become increasingly dependent on Jesus and less anxious. Before we get into the inner-life of a pastor, let's talk about the elephant in the room: Why is it so hard to be a non-anxious pastor? I believe there are some very important reasons to consider.

There's Too Much To Do

Remember that list from chapter 2 about all the things that pastors are worried about? That's just the beginning. The one unalterable fact about any ministry job, but especially the pastoral job, is that there are an unlimited number of things you can be doing and probably should be doing. The pastor is expected to be the main leader in any and all things. I received a phone call today from a wonderful parishioner who was putting the church down as a beneficiary in her will. She wanted to make sure I knew what to do when the day came so I could go into her bank and provide all the legal documents and such so the church could receive the money. I told her how awesome it was that she was doing that, but that I actually don't handle the money for the church, and passed the phone on to our financial secretary. However, the expectation that the pastor as the "head honcho" is overseeing and doing everything is not too far off base. Even if the pastor doesn't do everything, the expectations tend to be there.

If you are a solo pastor it's not far-fetched to see yourself designing bulletins, setting out communion, printing songs for the worship team, doing pastoral visitations, calling volunteers, etc. This is on top of the basic aspect of the job. The pastor that has a staff won't be doing all that, but will be adding other things to the schedule like staff meetings, mentoring, staff relations, organizational charts, etc. We haven't even gotten into the parts of the position that are universal, like preaching and teaching. With a plate that full, it's hard not to be a bit anxious and worried about the "many things" that Martha said were in front of her. They are in front of every pastor.

The Pastor is a Human

The calling of a pastor doesn't make the pastor immune to the problems and pains of the world. Many would even argue that the pastor is more exposed and more likely to be affected by the problems and pains of the world. However, it's not only the exposure and even the spiritual warfare that may come towards a pastor that affects; it is the reality that a pastor steps into the mantle of pastor not as a blank slate, but with life already behind him/her. Before stepping into the pulpit that first week, the pastor has grown from a baby to an adult and in that time, this pastor has experienced what life has thrown at them. The hardships of life aren't spared from a pastor in their own upbringing: the pains, sorrows, frustrations, loneliness, rejection, and insecurities.

This means that a pastor comes to their new vocation with the same inner anxiety as anyone else would. At this point we need to turn to Henri Nouwen who wrote *The Wounded Healer*, a book entirely about this very reality: the pastor as a human stepping into, and living into their vocation. I wish I could quote the majority of the book for this section, but instead, I'll pull out a few very important quotes that illustrate the struggle of a pastor, especially the pastor struggling to be a non-anxious leader. "For the minister is called to recognize the sufferings of his time in his own heart and make that recognition the starting point of his service. Whether he tries to enter into a dislocated world, relate to a convulsive generation, or speak to a dying man, his service will not be perceived as authentic unless it comes from a heart wounded by the suffering about which he speaks."[1]

Nouwen describes the suffering of a pastor not as something to run from but something to embrace in the shepherding of their people. However, he says it's important for the pastor to recognize the workings of their own soul. "The man who can articulate the movements of his inner life, who can give names to his varied experiences, need no longer be a victim of himself, but is able slowly and consistently to remove the obstacles that prevent the spirit from entering. He is able to create space for Him whose heart is greater than his, whose eyes see more than his, and whose hands can heal more than his."[2]

Like a guide on a trail we've never traversed, Nouwen helps the pastor understand that the wounds are there and we can't pretend that they are not. Instead, we need to walk through them, understand them, and even use them for the glory of God. This will create pathways of empathy for our task of loving our people well.

One more quote from Nouwen will suffice to finish this point; "The first and most basic task of the minister of tomorrow is to clarify the immense confusion which can arise when people enter this new internal world. It is a painful fact indeed to realize how poorly prepared most Christian leaders prove to be when they are invited to be spiritual leaders in the true sense.

---

1. Nouwen, *The Wounded Healer*, XVI
2. Nouwen, *The Wounded Healer*, 38.

Most of them are used to thinking in terms of large-scale organization, getting people together in churches . . . running the show as a circus director. They have become unfamiliar with, and even somewhat afraid of, the deep and significant movements of the Spirit. I am afraid that in a few decades the Church will be accused of having failed in its most basic task: to offer men creative ways to communicate with the source of human life."[3]

When we are able to sit with Jesus as Mary did, we can then teach other people to do the same. We talked about anxious pastors who bring people into the house and set them before Jesus but then rush off to the kitchen to keep doing the preparations. In this scenario, imagine the pastor's role as walking people to the feet of Jesus and sitting there with them. They can then help seekers understand some of these amazing things Jesus is saying and doing.

Let's go back to the text for a minute in Luke 10:39. We see that while Martha is the main character in the story, Mary is about to steal the spotlight, accidentally. "She had a sister called Mary, who sat at the Lord's feet listening to what he said." The way Luke wrote this account is fascinating because it's as if he understood that people would either be familiar with Martha or would naturally assume she's the main character in the kingdom of God because she's the "hostess with the mostest." So, he casually says, she had a sister called Mary. In the kingdom of God, the people we think will be the main characters are usually not, and those we think are background characters become the main characters. Luke illustrates this point well. We align ourselves with important people and important churches and important ministries, and yet in the kingdom of God, it is all flipped upside down. In the new heavens and new earth where we'll all be eating the big feast with Jesus, the celebrity pastors won't have the spotlight. It'll be these non-anxious pastors who you wouldn't have realized were there before.

Pastors who sit at the feet of Jesus are going against the grain of what the world, and maybe even their own churches are pushing them to do. I can imagine Mary feeling a little shame and condemnation when her sister steps into the room and demands that Jesus sends her to help. Her thoughts may have been, W*hoops! I probably should have been helping. That's the expectation of me, but Jesus' stories are just so good.* She may have started to stand up and dust herself off, because her sister was right, until Jesus says something remarkable to them. "Mary has chosen what is better, and it will

---

3. Nouwen, *The Wounded Healer*, 38.

not be taken from her." Mary quickly sits back down to soak in some more stories and teachings from Jesus.

The World is Anxious

If you are desiring to be a non-anxious pastor, you will have people who will step into the room and demand that you do more, say more, perform more, plan more, and get busier. However, if you are truly waiting on the Lord and not just being lazy, "this won't be taken from you." The way the world works is by cultivating enough inner anxiety to keep the machine turning, so you buy the products you are supposed to, check your phone constantly, turn on the news every evening, update your social media accounts consistently, work more hours, yell in rush hour, etc. The world is perceived to revolve around you and yet disappointingly, not around you at the same time. You are to look out for number one, but not when it gets in the way of others.

The pastoral vocation in an anxious world is to be self-aggrandizing, and yet in the "care for others" way as much as possible. The pastor is caught in a web of trying to look cool, be cool, preach cool, but to do it in a way so as to also look loving. It's nearly impossible, especially if you are to nurture the inner life too.

Jesus teaches us a lesson here by commenting on the act of Mary sitting at his feet. The posture of sitting at someone else's feet is surrender. It's a submissive act when you accept your place below because they know more than you. The only times we see sitting at someone else's feet in our society is when an apprentice is learning a trade, in school, or has a mentor. And this is exactly the point—we have chosen to be a disciple. To apprentice under them. You can't learn under someone by being off and busy somewhere else. You have to sit at their feet.

Feet aren't idle. Feet aren't meant to always be positioned below a chair. They are meant to walk and go places. This is exactly what Jesus' feet did. He didn't forever sit at Martha's house; he walked all over the place and it is very likely that Mary (and probably even Martha) were among the women who followed him.[4]

The act of following someone else is to admit you don't know the way. What's frustrating for most leaders as they sit with Jesus and follow him is that it seems he should be moving. We are having to sit. When it seems he should be sitting, he's moving and we are walking into uncomfortable

---

4. Matthew 27:55

situations of leadership. Karl Clifton-Soderstrom in his book, *The Cardinal and The Deadly* describes this well when he says that the virtue of faith and the vice of sloth actually are on the same hinge. That hinge is the ability to receive divine grace. "When the vice of sloth takes root in the soul, like pride, it fixates the individual on one's own self and away from God. Whereas pride wrongly considers the self its own salvation and source of triumph, sloth burdens the person with one's own emptiness, leaving him or her with the sheer banality of everyday life."[5] He goes on to say, "Faith is thus fundamentally the virtue whereby, paradoxically, we excel in our dependence on God."[6]

To apply the point of Clifton-Soderstrom into our task at hand, a non-anxious church isn't slothful, as this would imply they are refusing to receive divine grace. Instead, a non-anxious church is motivated through the virtue of faith, receiving divine grace by the bucketful.

The reality of following Jesus is you can't lead him. You can surrender and let him lead you but you can't lead him. He is the Good Shepherd who knows the way. Think of how we are led in Psalm 23:

> The Lord is my shepherd, I lack nothing.
> He makes me lie down in green pastures, he leads me beside quiet waters, he refreshes my soul.
> He guides me along the right paths for his name's sake.
> Even though I walk through the darkest valley, I will fear no evil, for you are with me; your rod and your staff, they comfort me.
> You prepare a table before me in the presence of my enemies.
> You anoint my head with oil; my cup overflows.
> Surely your goodness and love will follow me all the days of my life, and I will dwell in the house of the Lord forever.

Where are we led when we follow the Good Shepherd according to this Psalm? Green pastures, quiet waters, right paths, dark valleys, tables with enemies, all the days of my life. This is fascinating because it sounds an awful lot like an analogy of life. Following Jesus through life means all of life including dark valleys and right paths. I also love how it says, "He makes me lie down," since in following Jesus sometimes we need to rest, and we need to trust that it's okay to rest right now. The shepherd isn't moving right now and so neither should we. These are the times when we will feel most anxious to move and are ready and eager to do so. However, we don't

---

5. Clifton-Soderstom, *The Cardinal and The Deadly*, 34.
6. Clifton-Soderstom, *The Cardinal and The Deadly*, 40.

know the way. Then there are times when he's walking and we may think it's time to turn back or to rest. When he starts leading us through the dark valley, I promise you, all of us begin to look for a route out of there thinking Jesus got himself lost. We will see a cleft on a cliff and think perhaps it's a way to climb out. Or a little path looks like it may lead to an escape from the valley and we will want to take it. The non-anxious Jesus keeps leading us through, and we have to decide if we should keep following. When we do—others will tell us we are walking when we shouldn't and then sitting when we should be running, because they won't see the hand of Jesus. But it's okay. Jesus is with us and we've "chosen what is better."

The World's Anxiety Comes Into the Church

It's difficult to be non-anxious because the anxiety of the world infiltrates the church. We will look at this closer in the next chapter, but as we analyze the non-anxious pastor we need to understand that the anxiety of the people and leaders in the church will come to the desk of the pastor. I saw a Twitter post from author and pastor John Starke that illustrated this well. He said, "Someone said at our elder meeting last night: 'When Jesus doesn't move fast enough and get things done, people will then want their pastors to move fast enough and get things done. And sometimes pastors will want to oblige.' And I just thought that was wise."[7]

This infiltration of anxiety has always been a reality and you can ask any pastor about it. They'll have countless stories, but COVID-19 made it alarmingly apparent. In the church where I pastor, I had countless comments come in about things that I should do and shouldn't do to respond to the pandemic; things that were contradictory to each other. We had people all over the map on it. However, the one thing they all had in common was the demand for the pastor to respond in some way. I bet if I had taken a poll of our congregation (at the time) most would have said I wasn't moving fast enough (in whichever direction they thought we should go).

It's hard for a pastor to become and remain a non-anxious pastor. What can we do to combat the anxiousness that is flooding our offices and lives? Let's take a look at what's on the inside.

---

7. Starke, Twitter post, April 20, 2021, 12:16pm.

NURTURING THE INNER LIFE

I think one of the biggest struggles for nurturing the inner life is that we think that it is something to put on our to-do list. We relegate it to its own time slot and maybe even a specific activity. Of course, there are disciplines and activities we can do to help develop our soul but we have to realize and come to understand that our inner life is being cultivated all the time in everything we say and do. Everywhere we go and every activity we participate in is fostering what is happening inside of us and thus one of the most helpful ways of developing our soul is paying attention to God's activity in all of life.

If "God-activity" isn't regulated to a specific day of the week or a specific program we attend, and we realize he is active with us while we brush our teeth and drive our kids to soccer, we will be developing the inner life. Harkening back to Psalm 23, we should learn to seek God in the green pastures as well as in the dark valleys and all the boring places in between. This is the work of being a disciple: sitting at the feet of Jesus and following where he leads at all times. If we are in a pit; where is God in this pit? If we are on the mountaintop; where is God on this mountaintop? If we are walking the same road we walk every single day; where is God on this road? We preach that Christ is in us, but do we recognize this reality? Understand that he is there in our routine, still working while we sleep, and whispering to us to come as we go about our frantic activity.

Jesus says that the two greatest tasks are to love God and love others. To love well we first have to be present with the one we are working to love. It's extremely hard to love someone well if you aren't present with them. A long-distance relationship takes the even more intentional discipline of being present through letters, phone calls, face-time, etc. In order to love God well we first have to understand he is present with us, and then we make ourselves present to him. To borrow from Brother Lawrence, this is "practicing the presence of God." And then to love others well we would be "practicing the presence of others."[8] This is the task of a disciple of Jesus and therefore this task needs to be modeled to the utmost by the pastor. Practice being present with God and practice being present with others. When we do both of these well we will develop an inner life that is loving of God and others.

---

8. Lawrence, *Practicing the Presence of God*.

At the church I pastor, our catchphrase is "With Jesus, Like Jesus," and every week we work this into the language we use; as followers of Jesus' way we want to be with Jesus and like Jesus. When we are *with* Jesus we will become more *like* Jesus. It starts with sitting at his feet and then when he gets up to go, tagging along. The inner life starts and develops from this place of being with Jesus. He is our example in his own life. The Scriptures record countless times when Jesus went off to an isolated place to pray. My favorite example comes from Mark 1:35-37 which says; "Very early in the morning, while it was still dark, Jesus got up, left the house and went off to a solitary place, where he prayed. Simon and his companions went to look for him, and when they found him, they exclaimed: 'Everyone is looking for you!'"

The "being with Jesus life" isn't going to just happen to fall into place. It's going to take, as Jesus shows us above, discipline; the act of getting up and making it happen. If you've been a Christian for any length of time you know that by nature, the anxious world around us is pulling us in like gravity, and we need to find the rhythms of Jesus' grace so as not to be sucked in. Therefore, a pastor must find a way to be both intentional and unintentional in their times with Jesus. By intentional, I mean rhythms and focused habits on being with Jesus. By unintentional I mean throughout the day spontaneously noticing how God is there.

There are many amazing teachers and books on this exact subject and each pastor will need to plan their way forward with where they are in life and what works for them. Some recommendations include creating a life rule, rhythms of sabbath, the daily office, devotional time, lectio divina, and many other great spiritual disciplines that cultivate a life with Jesus.

This learning to be with Jesus as a human and as a pastor will help you learn to hear his voice, to wait on him when it's time to wait, and joyfully run when it's time to run. It will create a deeper faith that he is the wise provider of all our needs. He cares about your congregation more than you do and will lead them where they need to go. Can you wait on him?

A life learned to be with Jesus will also help create a deeper dependence, knowing that he has been faithful in the past, is currently faithful, and promises to be faithful in the future. This faithfulness is unchanging; it has never failed and it won't start now. For this reason, you can depend on him no matter what storm is raging around you. Don't just preach this sermon; live this truth as the non-anxious pastor that your church needs. They are looking to the pastor to show them what it looks like to be like Jesus: non-anxious in an anxious world. Maybe this is what Jesus meant when he said: "Can the blind lead the blind? Will they not both fall into a pit?"[9] If you are an anxious pastor, but trying to lead the church to non-anxiousness won't you both fall in a pit?

Instead, Jesus says; "The student is not above the teacher, but everyone who is fully trained will be like their teacher."[10] The pastor is to be the first student at the feet of the best teacher, Jesus. He will lead, if we will only follow. He will speak if only we will listen. And what do pastors struggle with when their own anxiety comes to the surface? Listening, both to God and to others. In pastoral counseling, the temptation is to talk more than listen, and in leading, the temptation is to get ahead of God.

Winn Collier in the Eugene Peterson biography records Peterson's advice to pastors as this: "I would want to tell pastors to quit being so busy and learn quiet, to quit talking so much and learn silence, to quit treating the congregation as customers and treat them with dignity as souls-in-formation. The primary thing that we are dealing with as pastors is the Word of God. And the primary stance we must learn both as pastors and congregations is to listen. There can be no language that works at all if someone is not listening. And since God is the primary voice in the gospel world, we pastors have to lead the way in listening, doing it ourselves and encouraging others to do it."[11] The hard part about all this is that it takes an inner strength which most of us struggle to embrace, to be this quiet and this patient. Our anxiety won't naturally allow other people's anxiety to steal the show.

Later in the same book, Collier records Peterson with more words for pastors. "Alarmed by the beguiling assumptions undergirding most church leadership trends, Eugene cautioned pastors that true ministry typically requires a pastor to operate from the margins. 'This is modest work. This is not glamorous work, this is behind-the-scenes, ignored, patient servant work. Forget about being relevant, about being effective. Friends, you are living in exile—get used to it . . . the less people notice you the better.'"[12]

Peterson helps us move into the next part of our inner work towards humility. He notes that the hardest work of all is being in the spotlight but remaining humble. Every week as a pastor you have people sitting at your feet, ready to hear from you for thirty or so minutes at a time. They will just

---

9. Luke 6:39
10. Luke 6:40
11. Collier, *A Burning in My Bones,* 238–239.
12. Collier, *A Burning in My Bones,* 270.

quietly listen to what you have to say. Then many will tell you at the door how much of a blessing it was and how much of a blessing you are to the church. This spotlight is intoxicating and it's because our souls are anxious for the light. But instead of latching on to the True Light, we take the imitation spotlight and its fleeting pleasures of applause.

In Daniel chapter 4, we have a very interesting account of King Nebuchadnezzar looking back on the astounding events in his life. The first was a dream of a tall and mighty tree that was soon to be chopped down. The stump was going to be chained up and he was then going to become insane. He woke up startled and alarmed by the vivid dream so he summed his wise men to interpret it for him, but only Daniel could. He told the King that the loss of his kingdom and of his mind was surely going to happen to him if he didn't change from his prideful ways.

As the story goes, King Nebuchadnezzar does not change his ways and the events take place exactly as he dreamed. He loses his throne and is put out of the city because he has become a lunatic. It's not until he repents and humbles himself before God that his mind and his kingship are restored. Even then, his return is fleeting since he isn't king for long. The story is startling in part because King Nebuchadnezzar is first shown in a dream what his pride will do to him if he doesn't change. He has a chance to change the course and the direction. Why didn't he? The dream is essentially saying, "Here is how your pride will destroy you . . . " He doesn't change course because this is how damaging pride is to our worldview, our view of life, our view of God, and our view of ourselves.

Pride whispers destructive thoughts in your ear. First, pride will say, "Surely it won't happen to me." If you believe because you are a pastor, too moral, and too important for something to happen to you—you won't safeguard yourself from what could happen and thus inevitably it will. Pastors who morally fail in ministry have this view: "Surely, it won't happen to me!" Pride is what creates this view.

The second destructive lie that pride tells you is a false reality that "Life is found here," or a similar line: "You deserve this." Pride will tell you that life is in power, fame, prestige, money, sex, position, pleasure, or whatever floats your boat. However, this is very important, the river of life doesn't flow through those places. Our pride tells us to search out life and life abundant in these deceptive places. Yet we will never be satisfied in those spots. Those experiences will only empty our soul, not fill it up. Anything in the list above will not give you life, but will only drain your life if you make it the source of life. I think we may know this, but sometimes we need to experience it firsthand to believe it. Henri Nouwen once said, "Somewhere deep in our hearts we already know that success, fame, influence, power, and money do not give us the inner joy and peace we crave."[13]

There is an overwhelming danger to the human soul under the spotlight of fame and/or power. Humans aren't meant for the platform or the spotlight. We may occupy these spaces, even be called to these places, but these aren't the places of life. The startling truth about the spotlight is that it doesn't energize a human soul. It only sucks it dry. The people who can handle fame the best are the ones who understand life isn't found in it. Those who can stand in the spotlight knowing it won't bring fulfillment are the ones who can handle some fame. Why do many famous people, much less pastors, fall? Because they weren't prepared for the intoxicating lure of the spotlight and had no safeguard against it. They didn't quite grasp the danger of the pulpit. Pastor H.B. Charles Jr. said it this way in his book *On Pastoring*, "If your spiritual devotion becomes a platform to be seen by people, when they see you, you have received the only reward you will get. God does not owe you anything . . . Jesus teaches that acts of devotion should be done in private, before God, not man . . . We are prone to preach to please those in the seats before us, rather than preaching as an act of worship to God. But we cannot overcome this temptation by moving the pulpit to our secret closets. Preaching is a public act of spiritual devotion . . . Let's face it: The pulpit is a dangerous place. It can fill the pastor with sinful pride that leads to his downfall. It can fill the pastor with discouragement that causes him to lose heart. It can fill the pastor with fear that leads him to prostrate his divine message for human approval."[14] I love how Charles identifies other ways the spotlight can drag you down: not just pride, but discouragement and fear too. It all comes from this belief that the spotlight is going to bring life, not destroy it. The pulpit is a powerful weapon against the enemy but it can also be a dangerous weapon against our own souls if we aren't prepared for temptation towards fame.

I like what writer Jon Acuff says about fame, "Fame sucks. You think it's going to be fun. You really do. Pop culture kind of paints this picture that it's the last great unattainable desire. To be somebody! To be seen! To be recognized! At the heart of it is an honest hope. We all want to be known. We want someone to know us completely and still love us. But that's actually

---

13. Nouwen, *The Selfless Way of Christ*, 34.
14. Charles, *On Pastoring*, 167–168.

the opposite of fame. Never confuse being known with being famous. They are not the same thing. When you are famous, people don't know the heart of you, they know the idea of you. They know the edited parts of you that you decide to share with the world. They know the shiny parts that make you look good. They know the manufactured you. Can you do good stuff with fame? Absolutely! But the challenge is that as soon as that famous person exists, you start to lean into it. It's only natural. It's so tempting to amplify the "idea" of you rather than wrestle with the "identity" of you."[15]

The Scriptures warn us against pride over and over and over again and yet—we humans need to hit our own head against the wall to find out it hurts. The Bible even tells us that God humbles the proud and raises up the humble. It says that pride goes before a fall.

The solution for pride is looking up to God, which is what King Nebuchadnezzar was inevitably forced to do. When we are prideful we are always looking down, seeing everyone beneath, making sure we are on top or headed that way. *Look at how high I am! How great I am! How important I am! How much I am needed!* While pride is about looking down, humility is about looking up, for to look up is to recognize and acknowledge that God is above you.

You're probably wanting to ask, is it bad if pastors are famous? Or if they have a big church or a large spotlight? No, but they need to be aware of the dangers of looking for the source of life in the wrong places, like money and fame. We need to realize neither are bad in and of themselves, but they both are dangerous to the human soul. Handle with care. In fact, Jesus doesn't teach us that having wealth is wrong, but dangerous. His ministry was funded mostly by wealthy women.[16]

He speaks frequently about handling wealth. What matters is how you view it and what you do with it. Take for example Luke 12:13–21. Jesus tells a parable about a man who had such a huge crop that he decided to build bigger barns to store it all so he could "take life easy." Then the man died that night. I truly believe Jesus used the crop analogy to show us that the man didn't cheat his way into this wealth, but also didn't earn it completely by his own doing. Crops come out of God's creation and in a significant sense, this wealth was given to him by God. The man decided to use it selfishly instead of sharing it. His view and use of wealth was way off base. Jesus would have been familiar with Deuteronomy 8:17–18, "You may say

---

15. Acuff, "Fame Sucks", lines 5–20.
16. Luke 8:1–3

to yourself, 'My power and the strength of my hands have produced this wealth for me.'" But remember the Lord your God, for it is he who gives you the ability to produce wealth, and so confirms his covenant, which he swore to your ancestors, as it is today." This chapter in Deuteronomy is all about not forgetting God. What's a major way to forget God? Gathering wealth! It's dangerous.

The same is true for garnering fame. If fame comes your way, it's how you view it and what you do with it that matters. Those who achieve fame should not want more nor should they live selfishly for their own glory but instead steward it well, and not be anxious for it. It's dangerous. How many people truly know how to handle it? It's as easy to forget God with fame as it is with money.

Pastor Rich Villodas had a wonderful talk about this very thing at the Qideas Forum in 2020. He spoke on the desire for celebrity and how it comes for humans, including pastors of big and small churches. He calls it celebrity-ism, something he says should be avoided. "Celebrity-ism is not found in the crowds, but in the soul and in the environments that reinforce it." And then he gave us four questions to deal with:

1. Have I wrestled with my entitlement?
2. Am I submitting myself to authority willingly, joyfully, and transparently?
3. Am I regularly proximate to people I'm not gaining any social capital from?
4. Am I living from the center of God's deep love?[17]

These questions used as correctives will be so helpful in forming our inner life as we journey towards being a non-anxious pastor. Villodas echoes beautifully the language of the Apostle Peter who says; "Humble yourselves, therefore, under God's mighty hand, that he may lift you up in due time. Cast all your anxiety on him because he cares for you. Be alert and of sober mind. Your enemy the devil prowls around like a roaring lion looking for someone to devour."[18]

Non-anxiousness may come, but then the task will be to walk in a way that you as a pastor can resiliently be Mary. We've been talking about this "Mary mindset" the entire way through, but we have to hammer it

---

17. Villodas, "The Failure of Celebrity Christianity."
18. 1 Peter 5:6–8

home. Becoming non-anxious isn't something you can check off your to-do list as a pastor. It's a constantly forming objective. It's a task that isn't easy and won't come or stay easily; we will have to continue to stay the course. To borrow from Eugene Peterson again, "it's a long obedience in the same direction." We need to avoid the temptations that will come to make us anxious again even if it doesn't look like anxiety at first.

There is more to be said about becoming a non-anxious pastor but we are at the point where we need to explore non-anxious congregations, non-anxious leadership, and finally talk about *becoming* a non-anxious church. If you are a pastor or want to be, or want to encourage your pastor, the next chapters will continue to help you on this journey.

Chapter 7

Non-Anxious Churches

I HAD THE AUDACITY one Sunday morning to stand before the congregation and proclaim this church gathering was an anxiety-free zone. I said, "take a deep breath because here you have no need to worry or be anxious about anything."

It sure is easy for a pastor to stand up there and say such things, but are they true? Is the gathering of the congregation, "the church service," the meeting together of believers free from anxiety? Probably not, but it should be because we are residents of a strong and unshakable kingdom as author and professor James Bryan Smith often says.[1]

There are many who would go so far as to say that the thought of attending a gathering of believers makes them feel anxious. *Will I be judged? Do they think they are better than me? Does this church just want my money? Will they force me to sign up for something? What if my kids hate the kids' ministry? Will this church perceive that I'm broken? What will they think of me then?*

Anxious churches don't help with the anxious attender and often they only compound the anxiety. *They seem to have an agenda. They don't seem to care about me as a person but me as a number. They are impressed with themselves. Maybe they expect perfection.* On and on the list goes. We looked into these anxious churches in chapter 2. So now we need to ask: What does a non-anxious church look like? For I assume if you've made it

---

1. Bryan-Smith, "Decision-Making with James Bryan-Smith."

this far you want to start progressing towards the goal of becoming one of those churches.

While our first thought will be to judge a non-anxious church by the outward appearance, you might assume that non-anxious churches are small, unassuming, probably with a boring preacher and a bunch of plain people. However, our assumptions won't always be reliable in this instance. Just like non-anxious pastors, non-anxious congregations function out of the inner life. These non-anxious churches may be big or little, city or rural, rich or poor. They may have a big staff or no staff, big budgets or little. While it may be harder for big churches to be non-anxious, it's certainly not impossible. While it may be a more dangerous endeavor for rich churches, it's not out of reach. And simply being a small or poor church doesn't make it a non-anxious church. I know many very small and/or poor churches that are very anxious churches.

Since we will be looking at becoming a non-anxious church in the final chapter, in this chapter I want to focus specifically on the characteristics of a non-anxious church. I believe there are ten essential traits of a non-anxious church. These ten attributes will need to be cultivated and protected for a church to remain so. What does it look like for a church to sit at the feet of Jesus? Its primary focus and attention is on Jesus. Paul actually talks about this when he is writing to one of the churches he pastors in Philippi, and in his closing remarks to the Philippians, he reminds and reinforces his thoughts which can also be applied to the church at large. Paul describes what he wants the church in Philippi to look like as he writes these words in Philippians 4:4–13:

> Rejoice in the Lord always. I will say it again: Rejoice! Let your gentleness be evident to all. The Lord is near. Do not be anxious about anything, but in every situation, by prayer and petition, with thanksgiving, present your requests to God. And the peace of God, which transcends all understanding, will guard your hearts and your minds in Christ Jesus. Finally, brothers and sisters, whatever is true, whatever is noble, whatever is right, whatever is pure, whatever is lovely, whatever is admirable—if anything is excellent or praiseworthy—think about such things. Whatever you have learned or received or heard from me, or seen in me—put it into practice. And the God of peace will be with you.
>
> I rejoiced greatly in the Lord that at last you renewed your concern for me. Indeed, you were concerned, but you had no opportunity to show it. I am not saying this because I am in need, for

> I have learned to be content whatever the circumstances. I know what it is to be in need, and I know what it is to have plenty. I have learned the secret of being content in any and every situation, whether well fed or hungry, whether living in plenty or in want. I can do all this through him who gives me strength.

There is so much in here that helps us understand what it looks like to be a non-anxious church. Notice the thrust of this section of Scripture. Paul is teaching them to rejoice in all things; not to be anxious. He's helping them locate the peace of God and explaining the way he's figured out how to be content so they can also be content. He is essentially shouting: *As a community of believers work on being a non-anxious church.*

This lays the groundwork for our understanding of what a non-anxious church looks like. While I sat and listed the attributes of a non-anxious church, I realized this list was not only overlapping Paul's words, but Philippians 4 articulated the non-anxious presence of a church much more clearly than my original list. The ten attributes a non-anxious church should embrace have all been pulled from the above portion of Paul's letter.

1. Non-anxious churches keep the focus in the right place. Phil 4:4.

"Rejoice in the Lord always. I will say it again: Rejoice!" This verse alone could have written the entire book you are reading. The word "rejoice" as used in this passage typically brings to mind singing songs or shouting acclamations. We use "rejoice" in everyday language to express things like, "He's rejoicing because his team won the World Series!" Or, "She's rejoicing over her acceptance into Stanford." Or, "They are rejoicing in the purchase of their new home." In this style of language, rejoicing is very circumstantial. We rejoice over things that happen to us or for us. We cheer, we shout, we sing. However, the greek word here, *chairo*, is from the word joy, but it means truly the state of well-being or placing ourselves into the state of well-being. This matters immensely, because while we can use the word rejoice for circumstantial wins, at a much deeper level it's about where you find your state of well-being.

If you find your state of well-being in your favorite sports team, life is going to have wins and many losses; especially if you are a Mariners fan, let me tell you. If you find your state of well-being in your acceptance to college, what happens if you don't get accepted? What about if you find your joy and well-being in a new house but you can't afford a new house? Paul tells us the place to find your state of well-being is in the Lord. Other parts of Scripture remind us that he is the only sure foundation. The only one who is faithful and sure, and who won't fail us or leave us. We can rejoice in such a Lord because he has never failed us and he never will.

However, let's think about the church. Where does your church find its state of well-being? Is it in the Lord? Or is it in attendance? Giving? Buildings? Community service? The Pastor? Anything besides Jesus is going to be a recipe for disaster, yet we see it over and over again. A non-anxious church finds its state of well-being in Jesus and only in Jesus. How do you know where you rejoice? Where do you put your focus? Or better yet, what do you celebrate? Because what a church celebrates is what they consider to be a win. What they celebrate is what they rejoice in. A few years ago, I was on staff at a church that talked about "celebrating what you want repeated," which is great as a statement, but is lived out terribly when only celebrating the anxiety-driven "successes." If we are celebrating heavily attended events, what happens when the events are no longer being attended? Or worse yet, what about the staff who are always expected to put on bigger and bigger events? Are they expected to keep on celebrating as they work to exhaustion?

We'll look at redefining success in the final chapter but for now, we need to understand that a non-anxious church will have their focus in the right place. They will rejoice in the Lord. Always. As in even when we've had problems? Even in the crisis? Even if the church has had to lay off staff or cut the budget? Always.

Always is important because a non-anxious church won't get caught up in the circumstances of life. They understand that if they continue to depend on God, continue to find their state of well-being in Him, the ebbs and flow of life will not destroy them. And even if God were to close the doors of the church, the non-anxious church can still rejoice for God is always God regardless.

2. Non-anxious churches are gentle and kind. Phil. 4:5.

"Let your gentleness be evident to all. The Lord is near." It's hard to be anxious and gentle at the same time. I'm not saying it's not possible but it's difficult. A truly gentle person has an air about them that is steady and comfortable with who they are and with life around them. Gentleness is not insisting on its own way. It's not pushy or showy. It's not flashy or aggressive.

Gentleness is soothing in a world full of hustle and bustle. What does a gentle church look like? They care about their people more than their program. They don't have an agenda they have to pursue over what God wants to do. They don't have to put on airs to show off to anyone. It's a church that is comfortable with who they are and patient with those who come through the doors.

Proverbs uses another fruit of the Spirit to talk about the way out of anxiety. It says, "Anxiety weighs down the heart, but a kind word cheers it up."[2] I love this imagery when it comes to churches. Think about all the people who walk through the doors as mentioned at the top of the chapter, anxious and nervous. It's the gentle and kind words of the church that draws them into this easy yoke of Jesus.

A non-anxious church is going to be kind, because it's hard to be kind and anxious at the same time. Anxiousness is much too busy to be kind. Anxiety is far too frustrated to consider a cheerful word to another person. If the drive of anxiousness is control and self-focus, gentleness and kindness actually push us in the other direction. We give up control and self-focus when we are truly being gentle and kind. What if we stirred in our churches the spirit of gentleness and kindness as an attack strategy against anxiety?

Maybe you're thinking, *Mark, wouldn't any of the fruit of the Spirit work here?* This may be part of the problem: that we don't see the fruit of the Spirit overflowing from our churches. When we look at the list of the fruit of the Spirit collectively we don't see enough in our church. Right? The other problem is that the fruit of the Spirit is not plural; it is singular—"fruit." Therefore, if the Spirit is producing fruit, it's producing a fruit which embodies all of these things: love, joy, peace, patience, kindness, goodness, faithfulness, gentleness, and self-control.[3]

I think if we focus on rejoicing in the Lord and exuding gentleness and kindness as a church, the rest will fall into place pretty nicely in the body of believers.

3. Non-anxious churches are prayerful. Phil. 4:6.

"Do not be anxious about anything, but in every situation, by prayer and petition, with thanksgiving, present your requests to God." This seems obvious, but let me tell you that anxious churches have little time for prayer.

2. Proverbs 12:25
3. Galatians 5:22–23

There is too much business to conduct. Prayers may be made before and after every meeting, but they in essence ask God to exit the room during the meeting. They, like Martha, offer Jesus a nice seat in the living room, maybe even serve him a warm cup of tea, but run off into the kitchen to prepare all the things that Jesus "requires." He's not invited into the preparations and no one even waits to see what Jesus might require of them. Prayerfulness changes this approach. It puts Jesus up front, in the middle, and at the end. It's "in every situation." What does it look like to have a business meeting, a budget meeting, or a leadership team meeting and sit at the feet of Jesus? Can a church pray without ceasing as Paul instructs the Thessalonian church?[4] He gives them this instruction right after saying "rejoice always,"[5] and right before "give thanks in all circumstances." It's almost like Paul has a method for these churches to be dependent on Jesus.

Now, while it may be obvious considering all that is said above, it needs to be stated clearly: Being prayerful doesn't mean being non-active. We can sometimes think of the prayer life as a non-active life. We think of prayerfulness as idleness. I once heard a pastor tell his staff that they never really get to any of the actual business of the church because all they do is spend the whole meeting time in prayer. Thus the budget is thrown together, the planning is dumped onto one person, and the leadership is very arbitrary. This is not what it means to be a non-anxious church. This only adds anxiousness to the church, not diminishes it. This sort of prayerfulness is avoidance clothed with spirituality. We pray and we go. We pray as we go. We pray and we lead. We pray as we lead.

4. Non-anxious churches are thankful. Phil. 4:6.

We didn't quite get all the way through verse 6 to the second part of that verse, which says, "with *thanksgiving*, present your requests to God." Anxiety and thankfulness don't do a good job of sharing the same bed. Anxiety consumes any other thoughts and attitudes. If we want to be thankful, we are going to have to retrain our self-centered thinking that aims arrows pointing in, to arrows aimed around and up. We look around at all there is to be thankful for, and we direct that thanksgiving to God. If an anxious church is always feeling an overwhelming desire for more, a non-anxious church is thankful for what they have.

4. 1 Thessalonians 5:17
5. 1 Thessalonians 5:16

When we pray as a church, even if we pray for more, we pray with thankfulness, reminding ourselves of how grateful we are to do what God has called us to do, to meet together as a family, and to encourage and equip each other. We come to focus on God and always somehow come away blessed. Our prayers look a lot more humble even if we are asking. Thankfulness comes out of the overflow of a life spent with Jesus. We can't be anything but thankful, while anxiousness comes out of the overflow of working on the preparations by ourselves.

5. Non-anxious churches make non-anxious decisions. Phil. 4:6–7.

Finally, the last part of verse six as we read just previously says to "present your requests to God." There are legitimate needs and things that are required of a church: serving the community, reaching the lost, preaching the word, etc. The performance model of Martha isn't far off. There are things that need to be done. Paul understands this and answers the question we all have; How do we sit at the feet of Jesus and yet make things happen? We bring those things that are required to the feet of Jesus. I love that Paul says that there's no need to be anxious, because you can bring God petitions. There's no need to be anxious, but instead, be thankful. There's no need to worry about our requests, but instead, we give them to God.

There's a prayer warrior in my congregation named Janey. She loves God and she loves to pray. She was on the leadership team ex-officio for many many years and when she wasn't ex-officio she was actually on the leadership team. Her purpose for being ex-officio was unquestionably to make sure we didn't make anxious decisions as a church. She frustrated the mess out of us, because it seemed like just when we were ready to pull the trigger on a decision, she would pipe in, "Have we prayed about it? I sure haven't. Let's table this until the next meeting and all of us need to make sure we are praying about it." And when we would want her to quickly pray she would always remind us that we didn't need to be in a hurry. The kingdom of God was never in a rush. There were times when we would come back from those two weeks away and the decision would be the exact same as it would have been if we had voted in the previous meeting, but the anxiety to make the decision was gone.

I learned a huge pastoral lesson from Janey: No matter how annoying it is, non-anxious churches should make non-anxious decisions. Even when I've prayed about a decision and our team has prayed about a decision,

I will often ask myself: "What is the non-anxious decision?" How many churches make bad hires because they are anxious to fill the hole in their staff? How many churches spend money unnecessarily because they think throwing money at something will help? How often do churches say yes to something simply so they don't have to linger on the decision long?

Now, I know you are thinking; *Churches are already the slowest moving group of people on the planet.* And my reply is simply; *that's not always a bad thing.* There's nothing more anxious than responding to the urgent. Jesus was never anxious and so never made anxious decisions. He never *felt* hurried and thus never *was* hurried. He took his time, to the point that Mary and Martha's brother died because of his lack of haste.

Jesus was informed in John 11 that his friend Lazarus was sick. Annoyingly, Jesus doesn't move. He gives some nice platitude about how the end won't be death for Lazarus. But the line that gets me here is in verses 5–6; "Now Jesus loved Martha and her sister and Lazarus. So when he heard that Lazarus was sick, he stayed where he was two more days." He loved them so much he didn't rush? Is this what Luke is implying? Wouldn't the opposite be true? When your loved one is sick, do you mildly say something cheesy and then wait two days before you call them or head to the hospital? No, that would be asinine. Yet, this is exactly what Jesus does. Why? Jesus is showing us something remarkable when it comes to leadership and the way of Jesus: that if we truly believe we live in an unshakeable kingdom and we truly believe that Jesus is the life, then even death itself cannot present anxiety in our lives.

The hardest part of this story and the toughest pill to swallow is the non-anxiousness of Jesus. The frustrating aspect of this story is that Jesus doesn't come right away and his reasoning isn't easy to swallow. They've brought the pain to Jesus. They've come in faith. And yet they wait. They wait so long that their brother dies. Jesus didn't come—and it's evident they know he could have but didn't. Martha in verse 21 and Mary in verse 32 say the same thing; "If you had only been here, my brother would not have died." What is Jesus doing? Does he not care? These are legitimate questions and questions you've probably asked in your own pain, your own frustration with the tardiness of Jesus.

What is Jesus doing? Where is He? Does He not care? We, along with Mary and Martha shout; "If you had only been here . . . " When Jesus seems to be late, we step in for Jesus. This is the church in our era. Jesus doesn't seem to be stepping in, so we will. We will make the decisions for him. We will find our own way out of this pit. "Through the valley? No thanks, I'll take this shortcut out of here."

We as leaders let our anxiety about death or even the possibility of it, control our decisions. When we do this though, we miss out on the life that is breathed into death. Jesus spoke and a dead man walked out of a grave. When we try to circumvent Jesus we don't get to see the miracles. When we lead with anxiousness instead of patience, we act like we know where we are going even though Jesus hasn't shown us the way.

Jesus can be painstakingly slow. Yet, we must wait on the Lord. This doesn't mean that every petition and request we bring before God will be answered in a definite way. He has gifted us with wisdom and ability to go the non-anxious way without his constant thump on the head. Though to do this we will need to quiet the noise. I love how verse 7 of Philippians 4 says; "And the peace of God, which transcends all understanding, will guard your hearts and your minds in Christ Jesus." Paul says present your requests and petitions to God. And you know what God will give you? Peace, which is better than understanding. This is almost laughable. What we need is understanding, but God gives us peace. What we need are answers, but what God gives us is peace. What we need are results, but God gives us peace, peace that will guard our hearts and minds in Christ Jesus. Sometimes we have to lead with non-anxiousness and the best answer we get is peace. And then we can proceed knowing that the God of peace is with us.

6. Non-anxious churches aren't looking for the next best thing. Phil 4:8.

If one of the struggles of an anxious church is always looking outwards for a new plan, new way to do church, a new strategy to bring in people, etc., the non-anxious church is going to be more firmly planted. This doesn't mean they won't ever do new things. In fact, I would argue that the church that is unwilling to change is also an anxiously motivated church. It's anxious about someone or something changing their precious traditions.

A non-anxious church instead will focus on plans, ways, and strategies that continue forward in the way of Jesus; the sitting at the feet of Jesus approach. Paul says to the Philippians that this looks like "whatever is true, whatever is noble, whatever is right, whatever is pure, whatever is lovely, whatever is admirable—if anything is excellent or praiseworthy—think about such things."⁶ What we focus on is important, and if we focus on true, noble, right, pure, lovely, admirable, excellent, and praiseworthy things, our church will thrive in what actually matters: making disciples in a non-anxious way.

If we are going to do a new event or an outreach or a sermon series, we need to ask ourselves if it fits the parameters of these focuses or is it another anxious way of pursuing our own platform and glory?

7. Non-anxious churches are natural learners. Phil. 4:9.

As Paul continues to expand on the focus of a disciple, there comes verse 9 which says, "Whatever you have learned or received or heard from me, or seen in me—put into practice. And the God of peace will be with you." Once again we see this idea of the God of peace accompanying something. This time it is the practice of sitting at the feet of a teacher. Paul is saying what he also says in 1 Corinthians 11:1; "Follow my example, as I follow the example of Christ." In other words, *See how I am sitting at the feet of my teacher Jesus. That's what you should do too! Let's all just sit here together. Go when he goes and sit when he sits.* The posture of being a learner is so important. While non-anxious churches aren't looking for the next best thing, neither are they consumed with being only inwardly focused. Non-anxious churches are wanting to learn and are humble enough to learn. They aren't seeking opportunities to teach but instead to learn.

The position of being learners means being comfortable sitting with other churches and learning from them. They are willing to help and work with other churches (even in the background). They aren't naturally competitive and recognize that the kingdom of God is not exclusively found in their church. They will learn from bigger churches and smaller churches, from churches of different ethnicities and different languages. An anxious church will be exclusive, tribal, and possessive. A non-anxious church will loosen the grip on their fist to give a handshake.

These non-anxious churches aren't trying to outdo the church down the road. They aren't gossiping about them or slandering them so that "my church looks better." They are wanting and eager to partner with other churches in town for the sake of the gospel, even if it costs them money and volunteers. They will do this without any strings attached or any glory coming back their way.

6. Philippians 4:8

8. Non-anxious churches aren't alarmed by a little mess. Phil. 4:10–11.

When Covid-19 first shut down the planet in March of 2020 we, like many churches went online and into smaller congregations and family groups. This season taught us many things as a church, especially about learning as you go, and never quite having a polished look. One of the first Sundays back in the building, we went to show a video announcement at the beginning of service. It started to play on the screen but there was no sound. I waited patiently like any good pastor but after about 2.7 seconds (not that I was counting), I turned around to look at the guy in the sound booth. He shrugged his shoulders at me as if to say, "I have no idea what's happening and I have no idea how to fix it." Not a great feeling as a pastor as the entire church just silently and awkwardly watches a video that has no sound. Finally, the tech team figured it out, but by that time we had watched the entire three-minute video without sound. There was a teenager at the computer and he didn't know that when the sound doesn't work you don't just play the whole video. Instead, you stop it and wait for the problem to be fixed. When the sound began to work we gave it another shot; watched the entire thing again. After it ended for the second time, a guy shouted out in our congregation, "*I liked it better the first time!*" The congregation burst out laughing and we moved right along. God bless that guy and his sense of humor because that's what it looks like to be a non-anxious church. Now I should admit that I was feeling very anxious and so was our worship director, but it only took one fun-loving guy to help us realize, *it's all good. Things happen.*

Paul says in verses 10 and 11; "I rejoiced greatly in the Lord that at last you renewed your concern for me. Indeed, you were concerned, but you had no opportunity to show it. I am not saying this because I am in need, for I have learned to be content whatever the circumstances." We will talk about how a non-anxious church is content in every circumstance but I want to focus on the other parts of this verse in this section. Paul is grateful to the Philippians that they were able to send missionary financial support again. They hadn't recently (maybe due to poverty or something else) and now they can again. Paul says they sent it because "they were concerned" for him. I love that Paul just glosses over his afflictions that cause their concern, since he is driving towards helping them learn about contentment in all things. However, Paul is in prison. He has been arrested, mistreated, maligned and so many other terrible things.[7] But he simply thanks them for their gift, the mess of his life not being the point of the passage. Yet they were concerned for his afflictions and wanted to help so Paul says that it's all good. Life is messy and we should learn to be content with that.

Here's the reality. Church is messy. It's the gathering of a bunch of imperfect humans trying to make some meaning of deep realities and offer themselves in worship. When we turn it into a production, sure humans can accomplish some amazing things, but in the end, we still aren't perfect. Mistakes will happen. Things won't always fall out as planned and non-anxious churches can't be alarmed when mistakes happen. We can't be disturbed when messy people say messy things. Non-anxious churches can't allow the pursuit of perfection to eliminate the reality of authenticity.

Non-anxious churches will let people be authentic, and not only in the way that makes the church look good. They will be willing to let professionals make mistakes. They will not be startled when a video won't play sound, not that a non-anxious church is eager for this type of thing to happen, but they are content in reality as it is. There's nothing more exhausting for people in church than when the leadership or congregation expects perfection. It's unattainable and unsustainable to pursue. If Jesus can offer grace, so should the church, and all the more in his power. Non-anxious churches will also be comfortable with young people and people in training to take the mic as they learn and grow. These churches are comfortable with a learning experience as people mature and grow in their gifting.

Take a deep breath. Your life isn't measured by your performance and neither is your church. You aren't defined by your best days nor your worst days. If there are people who don't want to come to your church because it isn't polished all the time, there's an anxious church up the street that is perfect for them. For the rest of us, I promise it will be better for your pursuit of non-anxiousness to allow things to be more authentic, which includes messiness.

This messiness also means that a non-anxious church is good at saying "I'm sorry" and "I forgive you." Churches that model repentance are showing each other what it looks like to sit at the feet of Jesus.

---

7. 2 Corinthians 11:23–30

9. Non-anxious churches learn to be content. Phil. 4:12–13.

Paul, throughout this entire section, has been building towards this idea of contentment, that in the kingdom of God there is no lack. Paul says, "I know what it is to be in need, and I know what it is to have plenty. I have learned the secret of being content in any and every situation, whether well fed or hungry, whether living in plenty or in want. I can do all this through him who gives me strength."[8]

One of the most popular verses to memorize and take out of context is Philippians 4:13. "I can do all this through him who gives me strength," often memorized as "all *things* through him who gives me strength." As a child, we imagine this means possibly flying and super strength. As a teenager, we like to imagine it as passing math tests. As an adult, we think of it as overcoming obstacles. But in context, the strength that Christ brings us is for the end result of contentment whether we have a lot or a little. Christ's strength is not for superpowers unless our superpower is looking at our circumstances and saying, *this is good, this is a gift too!*

Paul is helping the Philippians learn that being in the kingdom of God isn't a state that's dependent on the circumstances of life, that contentment is found regardless of the situations we face. We can know that we are secure in God and he is still our refuge and strength. What if we thought of this concept as a church? Sure we teach our people to believe this, but what if we truly were content as a church? What if the current amount of money the church has in its budget is all it ever has in its budget? Is that enough for your church? Can you still be healthy and growing in other ways? What if the current number of people is all you'll ever have? Is that good? Can you still be healthy and growing in other ways? Let's take it deeper. What if you have less money and fewer people? Could you still find contentment?

Now let me say something very important. Contentment doesn't mean you aren't trying. Paul doesn't say, *You should desire to be hungry*. He doesn't say, *You should desire to be poor*. He says, *You can still find contentment in it. Whatever your lot*. So, as a church - of course, you can and should do outreach to see more people come to church. Of course, you can, and at times, even should pray for the full cup, but a non-anxious church is going to be a church content with where they are and where God is taking them, whether with thousands in the seats or tens. Whether with millions in the

---

8. Philippians 4:12

budget or hundreds. The non-anxious church is following God and content with his gifts whether well-fed or hungry.

One litmus test to gauge your ability to accomplish this as a church is being able to bless someone without the expectation that it will result in higher attendance, more money, or the ability to show off. Many anxious churches will try to shower a new person with gifts in the hopes they will become a new attender. Or they'll woo a prospective family that's church shopping with the hopes they will become givers. Or they might even bless a family that is down and out with the intention of crafting an excellent sermon illustration or social media post to highlight how awesome the church is. This is a sign of discontent. It's not to say you can never give a gift or have sermon illustrations from helping someone, but if the goal is to be a blessing, then be a blessing; no agendas, no schemes, no strings. Just love people well no matter what. Be content.

Be content with outreaches that don't increase attendance, but instead bless the community. At the same time be content with outreaches that do increase attendance. The outreach was because Jesus asked you to reach out. You didn't do it for your own glory and the church's fame.

10. Non-anxious churches live in the tension of diversity.

The final attribute of a non-anxious church comes to us from the context of the church in Philippi itself. Paul is writing all this to a church that is embroiled in diversity issues. Throughout the entire letter, Paul's primary focus is on the unity of the church. In chapter 1 we see divisions between different groups.[9] We see this again in chapter 2.[10] These people are listed as being selfish and only concerned about their own agendas.[11] Chapter 3 seems to indicate a debate over circumcision and the law.[12] We see Euodia and Syntyche in such a strong disagreement that Paul has to call them out by name (for all of history to know) in hopes of their reconciliation.[13]

The diversity of this early church is complex, for as the *Dictionary of Paul and His Letters* explains; " . . . names such as Epaphroditus, Euodia, Syntyche, and Clement all mentioned by Paul as members of this church

9. Philippians 1:27
10. Philippians 2:2
11. Philippians 2:3–4
12. Philippians 3:2–3
13. Philippians 4:2

indicate that this first Christian church on European soil was made up largely of Greeks. Furthermore, it is safe to infer that from its inception women played an important role in this church, even in its leadership . . . It is a fact worthy of note that of the four Philippians mentioned by name in this letter, two of them are women and are designated by Paul as women who worked hard alongside him in the proclamation of the gospel."[14]

We know from Acts that the first Philippian convert was Lydia and then her household.[15] Acts 16 also mentions a Roman soldier as one of these early converts.[16] There would have been other Romans there as Philippi was primarily inhabited at this period by Romans, since it was a major outpost for the empire. As mentioned above there are plenty of Greeks. We know from the debates about circumcision that there were at least some Jews as part of this early church. This is about as ethnically diverse as a church can get in the first century: Romans, Greeks, and Jews all gathered for worshipping Jesus. We also can see in the letter that it was diverse economically too.

This means that the church in Philippi was seeking to be a non-anxious church with all this going on and all these discussions behind the scenes. Think about these early debates that we know took place and others we assume were likely to:

- Rich or poor, which is better in the kingdom of God?
- Roman-style church? Greek? Jewish?
- Circumcision? Is it for everyone or just the Jews?
- Women in leadership?
- Styles of worship?
- Location of worship, in the richer districts or poorer?
- Who is the guest of honor? What does that look like in this new Christian way?
- Differences between house churches?

Paul mentions specifically the self-seeking in the congregation and we can relate. The letter addresses a debate between two women leaders and we can relate. How does a church stay non-anxious with all of this in mind? This is what Paul's goal is as he closes his letter in chapter 4. However, I

14. Hawthorne and Martin, *Dictionary of Paul and His Letters*, 708.
15. Acts 16:11–15
16. Acts 16:29–34

think he would summarize it by saying what he told Euodia and Syntyche, "... to be of the same mind in the Lord."[17]

A non-anxious church is not going to pursue the natural tendency to be an echo chamber. We want people to have differences of thought, belief, political opinions, cultural backgrounds, ethnicities, languages, opinions, economics, etc. Trillia Newbell writes about how the Church should pursue diversity in her book *United*. She says, "God loves diversity. Diversity has been on display from the moment He began creating the world . . . And God shows His ultimate love for diversity in the cross of Christ; Christ died for *every* tongue and tribe, and on the last day *every* tribe and tongue will be represented worshiping Him."[18]

It's hard to lead a church that's diverse but it's worth it because it is the way of Jesus. It is much easier just getting together a bunch of people that think like you, speak like you, and vote like you. However, this isn't the way of the early church.

I want you to be honest as you evaluate your church. Think of those ten attributes of non-anxious churches again:

1. Keep the Focus in the Right Place
2. Gentle and Kind
3. Prayerful
4. Thankful
5. Make Non-Anxious Decisions
6. Aren't Looking for the Next Best Thing
7. Natural Learners
8. Aren't Alarmed by a Little Mess
9. Learn to be Content
10. Live in the Tension of Diversity

If you had to go through one by one and give your church a grade on each, how would it rate? Where can you improve? You can do this exact exercise in the back of the book (Appendix 1). Go through it with your staff, leadership, volunteers, and see how you do.

---

17. Philippians 4:2
18. Newbell, *United*, 126.

Chapter 8

Non-Anxious Leadership

I HAD AN INTENSIVE summer class for my MDiv that was focused around spiritual disciplines. At the time, I felt like this class was a pretty big waste of time. I flew into Chicago, left my young family back at home, had to arrange a guest preacher at the church, and hand off my other weekly responsibilities, and there I was for a week learning about journaling and being quiet. It seems that if I was going to give up my time like that, I needed to be doing something much more productive: deep learning, research in the library, maybe connecting with important faculty. Instead, I was sitting on a park bench for an hour counting down the minutes left to head back to class and explain to the professor why this class was wasting my time and everyone else's.

There I was, sitting by myself on this bench with the assignment to simply be quiet, practicing the discipline of silence and solitude. All I could hear were the noises of Chicago: construction up the road, kids playing nearby, cars driving by, people walking to classes. I tried praying but I kept thinking about all the other things I could be doing, I *should* be doing! I'm getting my Masters for goodness sake, and here they are, taking my money and wasting my time. Preaching, talking, conversations, lectures, that's what I needed and expected. I was acting out in real time the quote by West African Priest Robert Sarah, "Our world no longer hears God because it is constantly speaking, at a devastating speed and volume, in order to say nothing."[1]

1. Sarah, *The Power of Silence*, 56.

This experience showed me something very important about leadership—you can't be anxious and sit still. It simply won't work. And thus, you can't be anxious and sit still at the feet of Jesus. Think about the last time you were anxious about something. What were you doing? Moving around. Pacing. Probably talking to yourself. Even if you are stubborn enough to sit still and be anxious, what is your mind doing? Moving. It's roaming from scenario to scenario, from thought to thought, from anxiousness to anxiousness. And if your mind is moving even though you are sitting still, you won't be able to listen to what Jesus is saying to you. As a result, your leadership will be birthed out of anxiety, not out of the presence and instructions of Jesus. To be a non-anxious leader we need to listen well to Jesus, patiently, expectantly, and joyfully.

This doesn't mean that my whole life is sitting on park benches watching birds. The assignment was for an hour and because of my own anxiety, I felt so unproductive and maybe that was the point. Do you know why celebrating the Sabbath is so important for Jews and Christians alike? It's so they realize that the world continues to move without them. You aren't holding it all together. You need to sleep. You need to rest, and when you do, the world goes on without you. This may spike your anxiety right now, but this is vital to understand if you want to be a non-anxious leader. Your productivity doesn't add anything to God. His kingdom is secure without your performance. The opposite is also important. We aren't *always* meant to rest. In fact, the command is that there are six days in which we work and one day in which we rest. Thus, most of our lives are still "productive," the majority of our days spent working. This adds the corrective to the natural pendulum swing. Priest Robert Sarah actually writes about the Mary and Martha story in the activity and inactivity context. He writes, "Jesus seems to sketch the outlines of a spiritual pedagogy; we should always make sure to be Mary before becoming Martha . . . Christ tenderly invites [Martha] to stop so as to return to her heart, the place of true welcome and the dwelling place of God's silent tenderness, from which she had been led away by the activity to which she was devoting herself so noisily. All activity must be preceded by an intense life of prayer, contemplation, seeking and listening to God's will."[2]

There are many people out there who think to be a Mary-like leader is never to move, never to stand up, never to work. However, to lead like Mary is to know when we are to sit at the feet of Jesus and when we are to follow

2. Sarah, *The Power of Silence*, 28.

him. We know when lunch is to be prepared and when we are supposed to take a deep breath and take a day off.

Consequently, our leadership is more about showing up and sacrificing than it is about running around or sitting around. In chapter 4, we talked about non-anxious pastors and even how to become a non-anxious pastor. The focus was primarily on the inner life of a pastor. I think we should now focus on some of the byproducts, or the fruit of a non-anxious leader and how to lead in a non-anxious way.

Let's look at another story of Mary of Bethany and see if we can learn more from her response to Jesus. This account is found in John 12:1–8:

> Six days before the Passover, Jesus came to Bethany, where Lazarus lived, whom Jesus had raised from the dead. Here a dinner was given in Jesus' honor. Martha served, while Lazarus was among those reclining at the table with him. Then Mary took about a pint of pure nard, an expensive perfume; she poured it on Jesus' feet and wiped his feet with her hair. And the house was filled with the fragrance of the perfume.
>
> But one of his disciples, Judas Iscariot, who was later to betray him, objected, "Why wasn't this perfume sold and the money given to the poor? It was worth a year's wages." He did not say this because he cared about the poor but because he was a thief; as keeper of the money bag, he used to help himself to what was put into it.
>
> "Leave her alone," Jesus replied. "It was intended that she should save this perfume for the day of my burial. You will always have the poor among you, but you will not always have me."

This is fascinating for our study on a few levels. Not only do we have the same two women again that we have been looking at through this entire book, but there are more elements in the story to help us understand their motivations and love for Jesus.

We need to first realize that this passage is not Martha vs. Mary; it's not a showdown between the two. In fact, Martha and Mary are portrayed very similarly here. Remember, Martha wasn't listed as serving in Luke 10, even though I'm sure Martha would have said that's what she was doing. The Scriptures called her "distracted by all the preparations." Here in John 12, we see this one line about her in verse 2: "Martha served." This is an important adjustment in the language.

Remember, it's not the doing that was wrong, it was the attitude of the heart. Out of the overflow of the heart we speak, act, and do things.[3] Being distracted by the preparations is the attitude of the heart that is focused on things and is self-seeking. Martha wanted to perform for Jesus. She was distracted by how things looked and more importantly how *she looked*. The act of serving is listed as a gift of the Holy Spirit. In other words, when we serve we aren't focused on ourselves but on others. We are motivated by love not by self-interest. This is key. Truly serving others in humility is not anxiously driven, but puts presence above performance.

In John 12, Martha shows up ready to use the gifts and skills God has hard-wired into her as a form of worship for Jesus. Not to show off for him, but truly to love him the best she can with all that she can. Martha served because that's how God created her. She is no longer distracted, but she is now a servant. This is the first thing we need to understand about being a non-anxious leader.

A NON-ANXIOUS LEADER IS MOTIVATED BY A HEART OF LOVE

Martha takes the background in this story and that's truly what a servant leader does. In some ways, it feels important that John made a point of mentioning her. However, the servant leader in her is fine working behind the scenes. She no longer is running into the room demanding that her free-spirited sister come in the kitchen and help. She is simply serving. This doesn't mean she doesn't want to prepare a good meal or make sure that people enjoy the party she is hosting, I'm sure those are still on her mind because who wants to serve at an event where everything is miserable? Everyone who serves cares immensely that things go well, and so can you in your leadership. The difference is showing up with a heart of love rather than a heart of "look at me."

Mary actually shows us a spirit similar to her sister's but it's with a very different personality and gift set here. Verse 3 says, "Then Mary took about a pint of pure nard, an expensive perfume; she poured it on Jesus' feet and wiped his feet with her hair. And the house was filled with the fragrance of the perfume." Mary, never one to miss an opportunity to be at Jesus' feet, this time is not learning, but serving him there. Jesus, the guest of honor, came with an empty stomach and dirty feet. One sister is handling

---

3. Luke 6:45

the former and the second sister is handling the latter, both motivated completely by a heart of love and the opportunity to serve. Notice the attitude though neither are stressed with their performance. But simply present where God has called them. Non-anxious leaders will be more concerned with being fully present rather than their performance.

Mary is neither sitting still nor is she running around. She is fully present, which allows her to fully love. She isn't thinking about all the other things she could be doing. She isn't thinking about all the other ways she could have used this pure nard. She isn't caught up in thoughts about what a waste of time, money, and resources this is. She's simply loving and she's simply present. Judas is the one who pulls out the complaint, "This is such a waste!" This is very convicting for me as I did the same thing at the top of this chapter with my quiet time on the bench. What a waste of time, money, and resources! I could have spent this in so many better ways.

Judas says in verse 5, "Why wasn't this perfume sold and the money given to the poor? It was a year's wages."[4] Yet, John wants us to know that Judas wasn't motivated by love, but by performance and self-love. John adds verse 6 which says, "He did not say this because he cared about the poor but because he was a thief; as keeper of the money bag, he used to help himself to what was put into it." Judas shows us that often our "This is such a waste!" is actually cloaking our self-interest; our own desire to perform, succeed, look good in the eyes of others, look good in the eyes of Jesus, etc. Judas brings up a good point, but a point that is not motivated by a heart of love. When I think back to my experience on the park bench, I realize it wasn't any different for me. *Spending time with Jesus was a waste of class time, and my money, as I'm paying for this. I could do this sort of thing on my own time!* And yet the motivation underneath was self-interest as a keeper of my own money bag and my own time bag. I didn't like using it on being fully present.

What about you? Do you find yourself motivated by a heart of love, or a heart of comfort, ease, self-interest, money, performance, power, prestige, etc.? If you want to grow in your ability to be a non-anxious leader, the first step is to nurture a heart of love.

Instead of pointing out Judas' selfish heart, Jesus says something that helps us learn how to embrace this path towards a heart of love. Verse 7

---

4. John 12:5

says, "'Leave her alone,' Jesus replied. 'It was intended that she should save this perfume for the day of my burial.'"[5]

Mary wasn't at all being wasteful; she was listening to the Spirit. God had told her at some point to set this perfume aside and save it for a time in which she would be asked to use it. The day had come and she was listening and she was ready. This listening leads us to explore the next attribute of a non-anxious leader.

A NON-ANXIOUS LEADER RECOGNIZES THE SPIRIT'S VOICE

A couple of chapters before this story Jesus tells us something very important for our discipleship journey. In John 10, Jesus is explaining to and chastising the Pharisees about truly following God by using an illustration of a shepherd and his sheep. John 10:4–5, "When he has brought out all his own, he goes on ahead of them, and his sheep follow him because they know his voice. But they will never follow a stranger; in fact, they will run away from him because they do not recognize a stranger's voice."

Sheep won't simply follow any voice they hear, but when they hear the voice of their shepherd they know to follow. If you've ever had a dog you know an animal can respond in this way. Now if you've ever owned a cat, there's a good chance this will not happen. Cats love to ignore all humans as they somehow think they sit at the top of the pyramid. You don't own a cat, a cat owns you. When I take our dog to a dog park and let him run off-leash, he does great. He may explore a little and do his own thing, but will come when it's time. At a dog park, there are many owners calling their dogs and yet my dog doesn't pay any attention to those people even though they may be saying the same things I am, whistling in similar ways, and jingling leashes for their dogs to come. My dog pays them no mind. Why? They aren't his family. But, when I call him, he comes running to my side, because he knows my voice and responds to it.

This is exactly what Jesus is talking about in John 10. If you follow Jesus, you will recognize his voice because you have learned to listen to it. You know what it sounds like and you know when He is most likely to speak. You know that if it's condemning and shaming, it's not Jesus speaking; for he says "there is now no condemnation for those who are in Christ Jesus"[6]

5. John 12:7
6. Romans 8:1

Just like at the dog park, in this world, there are many voices calling out. Many may sound similar at first, but it's not Jesus. There are a lot of voices wanting you to go this way or that way. You even have your own internal voice that wants you to chase that squirrel over there, but when you hear the whistle of the one who loves you and has brought you into his family, you come running.

The longer you follow Jesus, the more you can recognize his voice. The longer the dog is in the family, the more comfortable it becomes with hearing its owner's voice. The puppy may not know who to listen to but the older dog does. This needs to be the truth for you as you follow Jesus too. It shouldn't be harder to hear Jesus as you grow up in his family, but sometimes it is because the other voices are so strong. The other voices are so much more anxious sounding and so it must be urgent. We *need* to respond to these voices and help them, right?

Mary teaches us again about non-anxious leadership. She had ready the pure nard she was told by the Spirit to save for Jesus' burial. A party happens to be at her house and the prompting comes; *It's time to clean his feet with the perfume.* Then Mary knows Jesus is going to his death because she was told this was to be saved for his burial. Through tears, and with her hair, she prepares him for what is coming next. The heart of love that listens to the Spirit is going to produce a wonderful non-anxious leader.

This is not to disregard the great sacrifice of Mary who gave this very valuable gift.

A NON-ANXIOUS LEADER SHOWS LOVE THROUGH SACRIFICE

As a teenager in high school, I had a good job and was able to save up a lot of money (for a teen that is). However, when I went to college, I really felt I was supposed to focus mainly on school and so I got an on-campus job a few hours a week. It was a miserable job, as two hours a day I would call prospective students and try to pitch them on coming to our university. In all likelihood, these teens only signed up to be on the list for the free t-shirt or bumper sticker. Most were confused and irritated that I was calling. I had plenty of sixteen and seventeen-year-olds hang up on me during this season; humbling to say the least. I was being paid minimum wage to cold-call high schoolers. It was awful. Every paycheck I received barely paid for what I needed to live, and I considered it hard-earned.

I was also a volunteer youth intern at a church neighboring the university during this time and regularly attended Sunday morning services there. I sat in the pew one morning with my Saturday night paycheck in my pocket, when I distinctly felt the Holy Spirit asking me to put my entire check into the offering. Granted it was probably only $125 but it felt like the difference between regular groceries and Top Ramen.

This is when I learned that sometimes the problem of being able to recognize the shepherd's voice is that there will be personal surrender involved. I wrestled with it through the whole service but eventually gave the whole thing up. I was hoping angels would descend in the middle of the sanctuary, blast their horns and tell everyone how amazing I was; how sacrificial I was being. In reality, there was zero fanfare and a bunch of cheap meals for the entire week.

I tell that story not to toot my own horn but to show that a heart of love that's learning to hear the voice of the Lord will at times find itself in a loving sacrificial position, which is where Mary finds herself in this story too.

Love will lead us to be sacrificial. Surrender and sacrifice are important attributes for a non-anxious leader to embody, for they produce in us self-denial. They allow us to die to self and live truly under the two greatest commandments: Love God and love others.[7] We have to get our selfishness out of the way first.

In 1937, Dietrich Bonhoeffer wrote, "When Christ calls a man, he bids him come and die."[8] It's important that a leader understands this reality on their journey with Jesus. Some people truly become Christian leaders as a means to a "better life." We even see this in the first century, reading in 1 Timothy 6:5 where Paul says that there are some who "think godliness is a means to financial gain." We need to understand that to follow Jesus means that not everything will always go our way, that following Jesus isn't always easy and that God isn't a celestial genie fulfilling all your wants and desires. Following Jesus is earth-shattering and paradigm-shifting.

This also doesn't mean that to follow Jesus will be constantly terrible, frustrating, and God will never do things that benefit you. C.S. Lewis probably had the best answer for this dilemma when he sought to answer the question; "Is the Christian way harder or easier?" He wrote: "The terrible thing, the almost impossible thing, is to hand over your whole self—all

---

7. Matthew 22:34–39
8. Bonhoeffer, *Cost of Discipleship*, 44.

your wishes and precautions—to Christ. But it is far easier than what we are all trying to do instead. For what we are trying to do is remain what we call 'ourselves,' to keep personal happiness as our great aim in life, and yet at the same time be 'good.' We are all trying to let our mind and heart go their own way—centered on money or pleasure or ambition—and hoping, in spite of this, to behave honestly and chastely and humbly. And that is exactly what Christ warned us you could not do."[9] What he's saying is that the Christian life is both harder and easier. It is easier because you have the "easy and light" way of Jesus, but it's much harder when it comes to sacrificing and surrendering. Self-denial is hard but it's worth it.

To operate in self-denial actually makes us live a fuller and more beautiful life. Jesus shows us the way to life is through death; that it is better to give than to receive; that joy is often found in the struggle. If Jesus truly knows the path to life, and defeats darkness, evil, and destruction, we will want to go that way.

Think of it this way—if your car begins to make a funny noise, you can simply turn up your radio so you don't hear it, or you can investigate. You go to the mechanic and he tells you that it will be $200 to fix and if you don't fix it, it may cost thousands down the road. You can choose to trust this mechanic or keep cranking up your radio. Which way is easier and which way is harder? It depends on if you have the end in mind or not, and if you trust that your mechanic knows your car better than you do.

Since anxiousness is an overflow of thinking and focusing on self, then sacrifice is flipping that script. If we are worried about how we will look, or who's the best, or feeling insecure, then we will run laps on the anxious treadmill. Sacrifice demands that we don't think of ourselves first, but God and others first. Then, instead of running on the anxious treadmill, we are sitting patiently at the feet of Jesus. However, this concept is the long game. If you want short-term results, be an anxious leader. You'll get lots of short-term results. If you want long-term results find the slower way that may cost upfront, but won't blow up on you in the end. Trust that Jesus knows your church better than you do. Trust that Jesus knows you better than you even know yourself. He is the master mechanic of your soul and the soul of your church. This is going to take two separate practices for us to embrace as leaders; being intentional and always abiding. Let's look at these before we move on.

---

9. Lewis, *Mere Christianity*, 197–198.

To sacrifice in the way of Jesus is not simply to throw ourselves around like we are on some roller coaster ride. There is deep intention to this practice. Notice that Jesus says of Mary's sacrifice that it was set aside. The sacrifice was intentional. It wasn't slapdash. She didn't see Jesus and think, *Oh shoot, I forgot a gift. Let me see . . . what do I have around here? What about this perfume that I probably will never wear. That'll work!* No, she set it aside and was waiting for the opportunity to sacrifice.

Sometimes we think that to be a sacrificial leader we need to constantly throw sacrifice at people and hope something sticks. Mary shows us that we need to be intentional and abiding. We only have so much we can realistically sacrifice (see next section) and so we do need to be intentional about it. Now, this doesn't mean that the Spirit won't speak to us in the moment and ask for something that we weren't planning at all. I'm sure this will happen because it has happened to me, but even in that there is intention. There is a moment where you step out in faith and cross the threshold from "I don't really want to" to "It's yours, God." That being said, what if we thought of ways in which we can be intentional with our gifts, talents, abilities, and resources. This would be game-changing especially when it comes out of a place of deep abiding.

Mary was abiding and listening for this moment to come to fruition. You can't be caught up in your own anxiousness and be intentionally abiding at the same time. God knows your talents, gifts, resources, and so if we are listening we will know when to use them *and* when not to. Which is where we turn now.

A NON-ANXIOUS LEADER KNOWS THEIR GIFTS AND THEIR LIMITS

Survival shows are fascinating to me. Probably one of my favorites—that no one ever talks about—was a show that only ran for two seasons titled, "Dude, You're Screwed." It was a program in which a group of survivalist friends would "kidnap" one of their number, blindfold them, and drop them in a remote place with only random things left in their care package. Sure, every now and then they would give them something really necessary, but mostly it was things that would make the friends laugh; like a giant pink bear or a set of golf clubs. Typically, the survivalist who was stranded would find a way to utilize those gag gifts to their friends' laughter and awe.

What made this show unique, besides providing more laughter than most survivalist shows, was that it also featured survivalists who were specialists in their fields. It demonstrated these experts not only utilizing their own abilities, talents, and gifts, but it also showed the limits of humans, (how long you can survive without water or food, or how long you can survive in extreme heat or cold) and it did an excellent job of revealing each survivalist's limits and knowledge. There was a scary scene when one survivalist decided he would travel at night, (to beat the heat) only to find that many other beasts traveled at night; beasts that would love to eat him. He simply didn't have that information about the area beforehand. He had to flee back to safety when he heard a lion roar.[10]

If I were dropped in the middle of nowhere, there's not a chance I could find my way out to safety in time. Even if they gave me a week's supply of all the essentials, I would need a guide, a map, a gallon of extra water, some Cliff Bars, and maybe even a medium pepperoni pizza. I know my abilities and my limits in this situation. I would fail and it wouldn't even be good TV.

There are two more truths to glean from this passage in John 12. Mary (and one could argue Martha too) knew her gifts. She also knew her limits.

Let's address our gifts and our limits. It's important to note that our sacrifice also has its limits and the God of love isn't going to ask you to sacrifice beyond what you can handle; emotionally, spiritually, or physically. God doesn't drop you into situations where He doesn't promise to be with you; not to say that it won't be a stretch or hard when you are asked to sacrifice, but that God isn't trying to burn you out. The survivalists were almost always able to make it out safely because their training and abilities helped them find the way. However, they almost all struggled through it, some on the brink of dehydration, heatstroke, starvation, and many other ailments. The reason it's called a limit is because it's literally the last line before something dangerous happens. Pastors and leaders have to know their limits in order to stay safe and not just survive but thrive.

Mary wasn't always pouring out perfume. I wasn't always giving my whole paycheck into the offering. These were both one-time stories of the Spirit's prodding. Humans have natural limits. There is only so much time in a day and there are only so many resources to spend. We literally can't sacrifice it all or we will end up exhausted and depleted. We shouldn't even try. God has more image-bearers than you. You are not the only one on the

---

10. Dude You're Screwed, "African Ambush"

planet, and therefore there is no reason for you to take all the burden on yourself. God has equipped each Christian with the Holy Spirit, and if all of these Christians each sacrifice where the Spirit leads, there will be plenty of resources to go around. It's crowdsourcing our sacrifice. It's engaging the whole priesthood of believers. This is important because there are many Christian leaders who think they need to be everywhere and do everything, whether it's because of an internal anxiousness to be needed, wanted, and accomplished, or it's an external anxiousness that is placed there by others. "The last pastor came over and visited me once a week!" "If you truly were a sacrificial leader you would shuttle me around whenever I need." Some people have so many expectations.

Read this clearly; you do not need to do everything and you cannot be everywhere. Protect your margin. Dr. Richard Swenson describes the concept in his book titled *Margin: Restoring Emotional, Physical, Financial and Time Reserves to Overloaded Lives*. He discussed reclaiming our margins; "Margin is the space that once existed between ourselves and our limits. Today we use margin just to get by." He says that, "Margin is a buffer, a leeway, a gap; the place we go to heal, to relate, to reflect, to recharge our batteries, to focus on the things that matter most."[11] Leaders need to protect their margin more than anyone else because there are more people demanding their time and resources. And naturally, as stated before, they are wanting to give of their resources.

Many people over the years have used the analogy of a bucket to describe this idea. The more we pour out of the bucket, the more we need to put in to keep the bucket stocked with water. If we always pour out more than we take in, we will eventually run out. Sadly, this is the story of many leaders and pastors.

Jesus practiced this spiritual discipline. He is known for his insistence on going off to a lonely place to pray. If Jesus, in his human existence, needed to find margin then we definitely need to follow suit. This brings us back to what we talked about at the top. Christian leaders know how to find the rhythm of rest and work. If they only work and never rest their lives will reflect this reality. If they only rest and never work, their lives will reflect this on the other extreme. Finding the rhythm between the two is ideal and the good news is this; God told us exactly what that rhythm is and how to follow it. He said for six days a week you shall work, and one day you shall

---

11. Swenson, *Margin*, Back Cover.

rest.[12] I think rest is hard for many leaders because to rest means to recognize our weaknesses. This recognition of our limits is such a healthy thing for Christian leaders to acknowledge. You have weaknesses and you need to embrace them. It's fun to focus on our gifts but we also need to realize that there are things you aren't gifted in.

As well as not being able to work every day for the rest of your life, you have other weaknesses. These need to be taken into account, not only to find ways to accommodate them but to be transparent in your humanity. You need God and you need others. Non-anxious leaders depend on both to lead well.

As we continue to talk about limits we are also going to begin to explore how non-anxious leaders know their gifts and walk in them. The conversation of limits isn't going away because part of our gifts is also knowing our limits, or where we are not gifted. It's knowing we have a jar of this perfume and not that perfume, or even that we have perfume and not a cash donation. We know what we have and we know how to use it, similar to the survivalists who knew how to turn a golf club into a hatchet. There are gifts and abilities that God has put in you and the Holy Spirit wants to draw them out of you.

Gifts are meant to also be used in connection with others. Sure, the lone survivalist is a cool TV show, but what made this show unique for me was seeing the different gifting in each of these people and how they used their own experiences to make the game harder and more challenging for each other. If they were all stranded together they could survive anything. In the church we are all to work together, using our gifts and abilities in conjunction with everyone in the church. This includes in the area of leadership.

A church needs a healthy team of decision-makers and influencers. You simply shouldn't, and can't do leadership alone. This healthy team needs to be a group of non-anxious leaders, and maybe this book can be a place to begin together on this journey. This group of leaders will all be gifted in unique ways. Their gifts will balance things out but also push others in their giftedness.

As we near the conclusion of this chapter, I can assume that if you made it this far in the book, you truly want to see your church become a non-anxious church. To make that a more certain reality you need to become a non-anxious leader and recruit a few more non-anxious leaders

---

12. Exodus 20:8–11

to lead others in this way. Develop a non-anxious team and this will spread to the rest of the congregation. It may be slow but it will happen, and even if the whole church doesn't shift towards non-anxiousness, the leaders will at least be in place to keep things grounded.

The reality of anxiousness is that it is contagious but so is non-anxiousness. This confidence in God has a tendency to be more caught than taught. Both anxiousness and non-anxiousness can be modeled, accepted, embraced, and incorporated into our lives and the life of the church. Which culture do you want to cultivate? It starts with each decision and each person making the decision.

Ask yourself, *What is the non-anxious decision?* And then you wait on the Lord. You can trust that He is working and moving even if you can't see it. You can trust that He is going in the right direction even if He seems lost. He was faithful yesterday, He is faithful today, and He will be faithful again tomorrow.

Chapter 9

Pastoring Anxious People

Stop! If you've jumped to this chapter before reading any of the rest of the book, stop and go back. I know this specific chapter is very much needed in our churches; however, we always think the anxiousness is out there and ours is mostly contained. We are great at rationalizing away our problems, and we are great at exposing other people's problems. However, to pastor anxious people well, we need to be on our own journey towards becoming a non-anxious person.

 Why? The anxiousness in someone else will expose our own and then the conversation will derail completely. Other people's anxiety has a way of igniting and spreading to you. It wants to speak for you and respond, challenge to challenge, insecurity to insecurity. However, letting your anxiety speak to their anxiety is like rubbing two matchsticks together and hoping it won't result in a fire. A great example of this happened when I was a few months into my new position as a lead pastor. At this point, I hadn't really established my own footing, but I had begun to feel good about where things were going. My newness and my pride were both openings for my own anxiousness to creep in. One of the staff members came to me because she was going to have a meeting with a person in our church who was bringing lots of "concerns" to her. I'm sure you know what I mean by "concerns." Yes, they were complaints. I told this staff member how to handle it and she was struck by my wisdom so she asked me to join the meeting. This is when I had the opportunity to keep up my "wise sage" persona by either declining or accepting. I accepted, deep down thinking I was going to amaze everyone in that meeting. The meeting came and went. We heard some complaints, I said some things, the staff member said some things, we prayed and the meeting was adjourned with no one feeling any better than we started. This wonderful staff member said to me, "Why didn't you do those things you told me to do before the meeting? It seems like you let this church member rattle you. You even got red in the face and defensive at one point." This staff member had me. I was busted. I let this congregant's anxiousness expose my own anxiousness and everyone left the meeting more uneasy than rested.

I learned a valuable lesson that day in pastoring anxious people. Mostly, that describes me too. So, to pastor these people towards Jesus, I need to effectively be on my way towards being a non-anxious person. Since I'll never fully be there, I should have been ready to keep my own anxiousness out of that meeting. I will save conversations about my own inner angst with mentors and spiritual directors. This is our first step in pastoring anxious people, knowing that every single person, pastor, leader, or volunteer has some inner angst and some quiet confidence for good or for ill. When we realize this truth, we look to the Scriptures and see Jesus pastoring anxious people. There are countless stories of those coming to Jesus with their restless spirit, some realizing it and others oblivious, and Jesus pastors them all.

Let's look at a few examples of Jesus pastoring anxious people to help us learn what it looks like to minister in such a way. Then we will explore how we can pastor these people in spite of our human limitations.

EVERYONE IS ON A UNIQUE JOURNEY

There's a story in The Gospel of John, chapter 4, that I imagine playing out like this:

As Jesus was passing through Samaria he took a break by a well to rest while his disciples went to get some food. As he was resting there, a woman who came around noon most days to draw water began her daily journey anticipating a lonely trip back and forth. Upon seeing Jesus she had to have been thinking, *Oh great, a Jewish man. One more person to send me judgy stares. At least he will probably ignore me and I'll be on my way. Don't make eye contact.* When she arrived, her hopes were dashed briefly when Jesus spoke; "Will you give me a drink?" Astonished that he was speaking to her and even more astonished he was willing to accept a drink from her, she replied; "You are a Jew and I am a Samaritan woman. How can you ask me for a drink?" John, the narrator, pauses the story for a second and reminds his readers in verse 9, "For Jews do not associate with Samaritans."

Jesus then turns the exchange into an understanding of living water and she begins to recognize there is something different about this Jewish man. Things get interesting in the exchange when the woman says, "Please give me some of this living water to drink." Jesus replies to her, "Go call your husband and come back." She presumably blushes and awkwardly replies, "I have no husband." It's not her singleness that she is blushing and awkward about. Jesus knows this and says, "You are right when you say you have no husband. The fact is, you have had five husbands, and the man you now have is not your husband. What you have just said is quite true."

The reasons for her loneliness, rejection, shame, are out in the open and for some reason, it isn't destroying her like she thought. Usually, when these things are said about her, it crushes her and she feels mocked, belittled, and rejected. Now, something is different about this Jewish man. She sees that he isn't like others. There are those men who seem to love the easy way she lives her life, and that always makes her feel strange and violated. Then there are those men who judge her with passing glances and contempt. She sees neither contempt nor lust in Jesus. The shame is in the open and it seems to sit in front of Jesus as a portion of her journey, more than the crushing weight of a grave being dug for her. Jesus seems to still think that even she can have living water. He seems to be more concerned with what's next than what's behind. For what is behind is what has been, but what is ahead is what will be. The encounter started with Jesus breaking down the societal barriers, continued with his non-judgmental looks and tone, and finished with his ability to know her journey in life completely and still offering her living water.

She couldn't believe it. The entire exchange probably only lasted a few minutes, but her life was dramatically changed. She came to the well with her anxiousness, coping mechanisms, and frustrations about the hand she was dealt. The people who come to church on a Sunday morning will also be carrying baggage and they want to know what you will do with it. Their anxiousness and even aggressiveness is a way of protecting themselves from what is within, and what they feel you will say, look at, or do to them.

She came to the well full of shame and condemnation. People will come to you full of shame and condemnation. They anticipate being judged and that may cause them to retreat or it may cause them to beat you to the punch by being aggressive. Their own journey has brought them to this point and you get to pastor them forward. Their past is what has been, but their future is what will be. This is important. This doesn't mean they shouldn't deal with their past, find healing from it, or confront it. Jesus, in fact, showed us this exact example. He put the woman's past out front, but when she recognized that life and life abundant was still hers for the taking, regardless of her past, it was freeing for her.

God brings people to church. He calls them and ushers them into his presence. He wants everyone to drink from the living water of Jesus Christ. We are responsible for helping them in this direction. Imagine if, like Jesus, we understand everyone is on a journey, and for better or worse, we are placed in this person's path.

We need to allow people to be human. We can't and shouldn't expect perfection from people, but need to be okay with the mess as people walk through life. The first step towards this future is empathy. The modern church is seriously lacking empathy, and we need to normalize it. Not sympathy. Sympathy is saying "There, there," with a nice pat on the back. Empathy is sitting down with the person in pain and weeping with them. Empathy is recognizing the pain whether it is valid or not and being a friend in the midst of that pain. Empathy is seeing the sin in someone else's life and recognizing that there is sin in my own life. We both need to run to Jesus. You need to show empathy to those who come at you, ready to take you down and throw you out. You are their enemy and they want to step all over your heart. This person is also on their own journey. You need to show empathy and grace for those who fail in front of you.

Jesus modeled this not only in John 4, as we saw above, but all throughout the Gospels. We constantly see Jesus meeting people where they are, and calling them forward in his grace and his truth.

OFTEN PEOPLE JUST NEED TO BE HEARD

If some of our anxiousness is caused by our longing to be accepted by others and some of our ways of expressing this anxiousness is by shouting and demanding attention, then maybe our pastoring should encompass allowing people to be heard. This obviously means in appropriate and beneficial ways for all involved.

We started the chapter with a story of listening to complaints and discovered the hard part of this task: People who are highly anxious in this overt way make us nervous and potentially bring out our own inner anxiousness. This could cause an explosion that is hard to undo in the church, and so we avoid these people and hope they leave. We pray for them to leave us alone and when we see them walking towards us we pretend to receive a very important phone call. Or is that just me?

All this reminds me of Luke 17:11–19; "Now on his way to Jerusalem, Jesus traveled along the border between Samaria and Galilee. As he was going into a village, ten men who had leprosy met him. They stood at a distance and called out in a loud voice, "Jesus, Master, have pity on us!" When he saw them, he said, "Go, show yourselves to the priests." And as they went, they were cleansed. One of them, when he saw he was healed, came back, praising God in a loud voice. He threw himself at Jesus' feet and thanked him—and he was a Samaritan. Jesus asked, "Were not all ten cleansed? Where are the other nine? Has no one returned to give praise to God except this foreigner?" Then he said to him, "Rise and go; your faith has made you well."

Here we have a story of a small group from a leper colony who has heard the news that Jesus can heal, even people like them. They are outcasts. They have been rejected by society and even by their own family. The disease was far too contagious to risk allowing them in the city and in the community, and so these bands of lepers would group together and depend on the kindness of others to survive. At the onset of leprosy they would have felt deep rejection and ridicule, people not wanting to be near them or to be touched by them. If they got close they would be told to leave.

The anxious people we pastor won't have leprosy, but they may have leprosy of the heart. They have been rejected and pushed aside. People avoid them and don't want to be around them. Whether it is their own fault, or the waves of life have pushed them to this point, they feel they can only be heard when they shout. Their rejection has caused them to be potentially troublesome, rude, annoying, and aggressive.

In the passage, the lepers are shouting because they are hoping against hope that someone will hear and listen to their plight. They are standing at a distance and yelling for Jesus. I love the line in verse 14 that says; "When [Jesus] saw them . . . " When I think of the anxious people that we get to pastor, I want to embrace Jesus' way of looking, so that I can see them, truly see them; not as rejected nor isolated; not as loud and audacious. Instead, I want to see them as humans that are in need of a journey towards healing.

This is exactly what happens in the story; Jesus sends them to show themselves to the priests and it says that "as they went, they were cleansed." Remember the point above? On their journey, they were healed. Let me add a statement to that last sentence: On their journey, they were healed because they listened to Jesus. The important truth is not that they were healed on any old journey. They were healed because they listened to Jesus and went down the road towards healing. Jesus saw them; he heard them; he instructed them towards a journey of healing. They all went, and they all were healed.

What does this look like for our process of ministering to anxious people? We need to see our parishioners as people on a journey in life. We need to give them space to be heard (in safe ways for them and for others and for yourself). We need to then help them take the next steps on their journey towards healing, whether that's therapy, removing anxious triggers, creating safer spaces, etc. While this is happening and before this is happening, we need to make sure we are listening to Jesus and allowing Jesus to lead them on the road towards health.

Perhaps the most remarkable part of all in the story is the lack of gratitude on the other side of this healing. This, I'll bet, is where most pastors preach from this passage, since Jesus is also a bit taken aback by the missing thankfulness. This is going to be true for us in our pastorate too as we help people on the journey and as we listen to their stories and lead them towards healing. Many may leave and never come back. Many may find health but never acknowledge your role in it. Jesus didn't then turn and remove their healing. He said "your faith has made you well," not "your thankfulness has made you well." It was the faith that set them on the journey. The thankfulness may or may not come. We sometimes are called to be a part of the healing process even though the road leads elsewhere. However, we don't need this praise, for our own journey towards non-anxiousness is not seeking out the approval and acclaim of others. But may all give "praise to God" in their journeys, as Jesus mentions in verse 18.

THE ISSUE ISN'T THE REAL ISSUE

One of the most consistent realities of anxious conversations is that the issue being expressed, discussed, and debated is often not the real issue that needs to be addressed. For example, when you get that nasty email that expresses frustration at your pastoral ability because you won't lead strongly from the pulpit about this latest political agenda (either side), realize that the political cause isn't the major driving force behind the email. They may not even realize this, but the issue at hand that they think is the end all be all, is only the symptom of the cold not the cold itself. Over-reactions to political issues could stem from idolatry, fear, or loss of power. It could even be familial tension or a number of other reasons.

This exact scenario has happened to me and I came to find out that a couple was taking their anger out on me because they were worried about their son. They had an adult son (who didn't even attend our church or even live in the same town) who was running as far away from them as possible, politically speaking, and they were worried that if the pastor didn't stand up against this sort of rebellion that I was allowing the entire congregation to fall down the same slippery slope. What they thought was a political issue really was family tension and a reconciliation issue. Honestly, I'm sure it was even more complex than that. Maybe their son was running away from them politically for a deeper reason than simply liking that political party, and maybe they were upset about his politics because they equated their version of politics to their version of Christianity. Could something unknown be lying underneath the surface of an aggressive attack by an anxious person?

When people want more hymns in the church it's typically because those songs bring such deep emotion to them and draw them closer to Christ. They want this for themselves and assume those exact songs that do it for them, will do the same for others, so why would you not want to sing them?

When people are upset that you canceled a program, this reaction usually comes from a place of nostalgia. That program either led them to the Lord or helped them further their own relationship with God. Or it used to be so successful and well-attended that they can't believe it is not now. It must be because the leadership isn't doing it right. The answer isn't to cancel, but to revive it.

These are only a few examples of some of the issues that aren't really the issue. The more complex the person, the more complex the real issue is. Remember Judas from John 12, when he told Jesus he was concerned about the poor?[1] But what does John tell us he was actually concerned with? Greed.[2] The anxiousness Judas expressed about what Mary was do-

---

1. John 12:5
2. John 12:6

ing was presented as one thing but it wasn't the real issue. He seemed so very concerned about the poor, and one would think that Jesus would also be concerned and would do something about it. The easiest solution for the duplicity here is; "Then dig up the root!" But that's not always what Jesus does; some people aren't ready for the roots to be pulled yet. Jesus pastored people first by knowing everyone is on a journey, and second by recognizing that everyone needs to be heard. These realities allowed him to respond to each person and issue individually. He doesn't say to Judas, "You greedy piece of work! How dare you act like you care about the poor!" It's John that gave us this nugget. Jesus simply addresses the issue as if it's a valid issue.

However, Jesus at other times does address the real issue. Think about when Peter, in Matthew 16:22-23, says that Jesus going to his death can never happen! Jesus rebukes him and says memorably; "Get behind me Satan!" What is more telling for our exploration is what Jesus says next; "You do not have in mind the concerns of God, but merely human concerns" Jesus sees into Peter's desires and sees more selfish thoughts than godly thoughts. I'll bet Peter wouldn't have been able to identify this ahead of time, saying his primary concern was not to see his Lord suffer. Jesus teaches Peter and us here, that suffering is sometimes the way of Jesus. And he teaches us that some people are ready to hear the harsh truth.

Jesus spoke to the "expressed" issue with Judas. He addressed the real issue with Peter. Remember the lepers in the last section? He responded to their desire for physical healing. Their need for deeper gratitude came further on in their journey.

When our anxious congregant comes to us demanding more hymns, it may not be the time to tell them that their real issue is misplaced nostalgia, that they need to be more like Mary and less like Judas. We shouldn't jump to that response for two major reasons. First, they may not be ready to walk that road yet. Second, they may be bringing up an issue you actually should consider. Maybe there is a need for more worship that crosses generations. There is another reality we need to come to understand. What are the real reasons we don't want to receive their concern? Maybe it's concern for them or maybe it's concern for "my way." The complexity of these realities need to always be thought through and prayed through with a non-anxious presence, keeping in front of us the truth that the person we are speaking with is on a journey and may desperately need to be heard. Rapid responses and quick reactions aren't the best approach to pastoring anxious people. It may help to tell someone that you want to pray about it and respond accordingly.

However, if you say this, you need to do it. This takes deep discernment and gathered wisdom from the Holy Spirit. A pastor should truly pray daily for wisdom and discernment in shepherding the people in their flock.

Pastors also need to know their role and calling. During the COVID-19 pandemic, pastors were expected to talk about politics, weighing in on every debate and every state's response to the pandemic. Pastors also were expected to talk about science, speaking to vaccines, social distancing, masks (effectiveness or not), and all the other science flying around. I decided early on I wasn't going to venture into these dangerous traps. I said the following to many people in conversation and in front of the congregation many times: "I am not a politician nor a scientist. I am a pastor and thus I won't speak in the place of a politician or a scientist but I will speak in the posture of a pastor." That's all I could offer people. If they wanted to talk about the Scriptural response to governing officials, I would do that but I couldn't stand in the place of a governing official since I wasn't called to that position nor was I residing in that seat. It turns out what my congregants really needed during the pandemic was a pastor. I was happy to be there for that purpose. Once again, the real issue wasn't the expressed issue.

Now that we've laid this groundwork for understanding how to pastor anxious people, we will turn to an issue that is absolutely maddening.

GROUP IDENTITY AND ANIMOSITY

Our perceived identity is almost entirely fostered out of community. We not only learn how we view ourselves by how others react to us, but we also explore our perceived identity through associating in groups, whether this is in families, clubs, political parties, churches, or sports teams, etc. Social scientists are constantly learning more about group identity and how it works, especially in regards to our exploration of our perceived identity through social media. A lot of our expressed anxiousness will come about through our perceived identity. I don't want to lose you here since these are loaded concepts. Let me support these ideas with the following:

In 1949, 1953, and 1954 a social scientist by the name of Muzafer Sherif ran a few experiments on group identity and animosity.[3] He titled the study "Experiments in Group Conflict" and gathered together very similar boys ages 11 or 12 years old who did not know each other. The goal was to pick boys who were very alike, so if these boys met outside of

---

3. Sherif, *Intergroup Conflict and Cooperation: The Robbers Cave Experiment*.

the experiments they would have most likely naturally grouped themselves together or gotten along well, having similar backgrounds and interests.[4]

The first study was conducted when he brought these boys to a summer camp in Connecticut. These boys were not aware this was a study and were fully ready to enjoy what they thought was a very normal summer camp. Sherif and his associates were the camp counselors and everything was set to explore group conflict.

After a few days of camp experience, these boys were split into two different groups and pitted against each other to compete in activities and contests. They were dubbed the "Bull Dogs" and the "Red Devils." The goal was to get them to start despising each other and start seeing the other group as truly "the other." It didn't work. They were fine with competing but they also would help each other out and work together to accomplish the goals and tasks. What the study was able to show was that by the end of the camp the majority of participants in each group identified people from their own group as their closest friends. Thus, group identity was formed. It wasn't a success in Sherif's mind, though, because he was unable to generate animosity. In fact, even the reality that 95 percent of the "Red Devils" and 87.7 percent of the "Bull Dogs" selected friends from their own group wasn't satisfactory for him because that means there was still a small percentage that made their close friends across the camp.

It wasn't until the 1954 study did he learn how to create the animosity he was looking for. The following is the infamous "Robbers Cave" experiment. This time when he brought these boys to camp he split the groups up before the camp and having never met, they were immediately isolated across a lake from each other. These were the "Eagles" and the "Rattlers." They were given the chance to bond with their own group and then after group identity was formed, they were introduced to the other group. The "Eagles" were made aware of these "Rattlers" and vice versa. They were told they would compete against the other for prizes and glory.

The groups began with taunting, but things got out of hand quickly when cabins were raided and flags were burned. The researchers then tried to help them towards conflict resolution by doing things like having a fun activity together. When this fun activity included food, it turned into an all-out food fight, with the Eagles and Rattlers assembling and battling.

What happened? In the first experimental camp, the boys found commonalities before being split into groups. Their primary group identity

---

4. Sherif, "Experiments in Group Conflict." 54–58.

wasn't with the formed teams, but with the overall campers. They saw the competition as a game and their rivals as their friends. They had developed a team identity with each other long before they were forced to reconsider this group identity. Then, when push came to shove, they were still able to see a fellow camper in their rival.

In the second experiment, this wasn't the case. The group identity was formed in a similar way, but only with campers at their particular camp. When they learned of another group of campers, these groups didn't see each other as fellow campers but only as rivals. They had never met and in their minds, they had no commonality. They were always the enemy and always would be the enemy.[5]

This means that before people ever come to your church, the majority of them have pre-formed group identities. Your church may not be the enemy, but your church certainly isn't part of this new person's perceived identity. They will subconsciously ask questions like; *Do I see myself as part of these people? Do these people seem like me or for me?*

The same questioning occurs in the congregation itself if the pastor is the new person; he is the outsider since the pastor was thrust into a leadership position without being part of the group before. The congregation is deciding if the pastor fits into the dimensions of how they think of themselves, how they naturally order themselves, and the current group hierarchy.

For church members, their primary group identity is their home church. They will do whatever it takes to protect that group and their perceived identity in that group. If the pastor/leader doesn't fit the mold it's only fitting to burn flags, taunt, and start spiritual food fights.

We need to understand something very important about how we work as humans. Animosity comes out of us the most when there is a threat towards our perceived identity. If this threatened person has power, it could get ugly. Maybe you are thinking, that's great and all but I don't have group identity, or at least not like that. Oh, but you do. You have a group identity. Actually, you are a card-carrying member of a few groups, and your allegiance to those groups matters a lot to you. To illustrate this point it would only take my telling you who I voted for in the 2020 Presidential Elections for you to write off this whole book if I happened to have voted differently than you. If I voted the same, you'd think, *I knew I liked him!* For some of you, this whole book is out the window if you disagree with this one point.

5. Mcleod, "Robbers Cave Experiment."

That's how strong your group identity is in your political party. Some of you are currently trying to decide if I'm one of "them" because you hadn't thought much about it to this point.

Or maybe if that doesn't do it, I could tell you my beliefs on women in ministry or infant baptism or Calvinism or maybe for you, it's seven literal days of creation! What's my stance on that? How about homosexuality? Speaking in tongues? A new one that's popped up is Critical Race Theory. What do I think of that you may want to know. For it or against it? And the list goes on and on. My decisions on these matters determine if I'm in your group or not. If I'm not, then it's time to burn my cabin or maybe this book. If I am, deep breath, you can battle side by side with me. Did I make you anxious about whether I'm in your group or not? I hope so, since that's how your congregants feel with their own group identities and associated anxieties.

This is why Jesus seemed to be a more "centered set" than a "bonded set" leader. A bonded set leader cares about the boundaries and who is in and who is out of their group. They care a lot about rules, regulations, litmus tests, and knowing if you are for or against their group. They create and/or demonstrate the boundaries. It gives them more control.

A centered set leader is more concerned with the direction a person is facing. Are you headed towards Jesus or away from Jesus? If every person is on a journey, what we should care most about is not whether they follow all the rules, but that their journey is leading towards Jesus, that their journey is allowing room for Jesus to lead them. The Holy Spirit can work out the sanctification and the moral side of things. We as leaders just want to help people take the next step in the right direction.

As we mentioned in the points above, Jesus was notorious for allowing people to be on a journey and he helped them find living water no matter where they had been. He also loved to break down group identity and reform it around him; the family of God.

Think of the story of the Good Samaritan. The enemy is the good guy and the good guys are the bad guys. Talk about how upsetting this story would have been for people's group identities. When a good Jewish man is robbed and beaten, all the good Jewish people pass by and won't help. It takes the Samaritan, the outsider to Judaism, to show mercy. The Rattler helped the Eagle when none of the other Eagles would. If this moment were in a movie our eyes may be a little wet here because the Eagle and the Rattler realized they were actually both campers all along. The Jewish man realized the Samaritan was actually his fellow human and neighbor all along.

Jesus wasn't going to play around with all the ways that humans like to group themselves. He wasn't trapped by their political discussions, their religious discussions, nor even their legal discussions. He always pointed people back to His Kingdom. The Kingdom of God is where we humans are supposed to belong. When someone comes at you with animosity fueled by their group identity, it won't be easy but you may need to be the Good Samaritan. You will have to find some commonality and work towards a loving next step for everyone.

One final warning before we move on to the next issue. There are churches that have learned about this group identity phenomenon, whether they call it that or not, and they've hijacked it for their purposes. They have become cult-like, and use group identity to keep people in check and aligned with their purposes. The goal of group identity is not to use it as a weapon but instead to be part of the body of Christ, always serving and loving one another well and working together for the common good of the gospel.

THE MOST FRUSTRATING OF PEOPLE

Finally, and maybe most importantly, to be a non-anxious pastor/leader and to pastor anxious people well, there may come a time when you have to let them go. Let me give you three scenarios to consider on this point:

1. Let Go of Those Trying to Leave

The group identity, the animosity, the toxicity, or maybe just the consumerism is too much and the best thing you can do is let them move on. I think some pastors try way too hard to retain some people who are trying so hard to leave.

Every pastor gets that threatening call or email that expresses this person/family is "leaving your church." You know what you do? Take a deep breath and give them the Aaronic blessing. "The Lord bless you and keep you; the Lord make his face shine on you and be gracious to you; the Lord turn his face toward you and give you peace."[6]

---

6. Numbers 6:24–26

2. There Will Always Be "EGRs"

I'm not sure if this is original to my mom or not. As a pastor's kid, I often would hear my mom refer to people she labeled "EGR." One day I inquired about this definition and she told me that it stands for "Extra Grace Required" and that there are certain people who need extra grace. Due to their own pain, frustrations, sins, shame, group identity, or what have you, the pastor/leader and other congregants are needing to give them more grace than others. Every church has EGRs and EGRs don't typically move around, though some do. This means there is someone in your congregation right now that God has put in this body and they need more attention, love, and grace. They may be the ankle on the body of Christ and they always seem to be a bit twisted. Give them a brace and love them well.

3. Church Discipline

There may be congregants who aren't trying to leave nor are they simply EGRs. They fall under the need of church discipline. There are so many good resources and books out there about church discipline, but the most important thing to do when it comes to church discipline is to not do it selfishly or maliciously. This means:

- Pray
- Walk through Matthew 18 in a healthy way. (Read *A Church Called Tov* by Scot McKnight and Laura Barringer about when Matthew 18 is used appropriately and when it is abused.)
- Operate in truth and love.
- Bring things in the light that need to be brought in the light.
- Protect any victims and families of victims.
- Don't do it alone. (We will get to this shortly.)

This section is a snapshot of the pathway for church discipline and it is not meant to be an exhaustive resource. Please find more resources, mentors, advice, denominational support if you are taking this pathway.

We should understand that Jesus pastored people by sometimes letting them go, and we never are quite sure if they made their way back. Take for example the story we often call the Rich Young Ruler in Matthew 19:16–22:

> Just then a man came up to Jesus and asked, "Teacher, what good thing must I do to get eternal life?" "Why do you ask me about what is good?" Jesus replied. "There is only One who is good. If you want to enter life, keep the commandments." "Which ones?" he inquired. Jesus replied, "You shall not murder, you shall not commit adultery, you shall not steal, you shall not give false testimony, honor your father and mother," and "love your neighbor as yourself." "All these I have kept," the young man said. "What do I still lack?" Jesus answered, "If you want to be perfect, go, sell your possessions and give to the poor, and you will have treasure in heaven. Then come, follow me." When the young man heard this, he went away sad, because he had great wealth.

Through Jesus' pastoral ministry this man "went away sad." He left Jesus because the teaching was too hard to embrace. Jesus didn't run after him nor try to make the surrender to himself easier. He didn't bribe him to at least give it two or three more tries. He simply lets the man continue on his journey. We may never know if that person came back or not. We only know he left.

There were other times when Jesus encouraged people to leave because they were following him for the wrong reasons. This is the situation in John 6. Jesus had fed the crowds and then crossed over the lake, but when he got to the other side, there the crowd was again. Jesus speaks to the crowd in verse 26; "Very truly I tell you, you are looking for me, not because you saw the signs I performed but because you ate the loaves and had your fill." Jesus tells them that they came to him again because of his performance and his snacks.

Then Jesus gets intentionally awkward when he begins teaching them about the true bread, he tells them, "I am the bread of life."[7] When the crowd begins to wonder about this teaching, he clarifies it by saying in verse 53; " . . . unless you eat the flesh of the Son of Man and drink his blood, you have no life in you." What's the response of the crowd and even his own disciples in verse 60? "This is a hard teaching. Who can accept it?" His teaching is hard and Jesus doesn't seem to be squirming at their discomfort, and then verse 66 says; "From this time many of his disciples turned back and no longer followed him." Jesus knew what he was doing. People were coming to him for his performance and his free food, so he began to teach them about food that is found through him. This became unpleasant when

---

7. John 6:35

he instructed them to eat his flesh and drink his blood. They didn't like it and they left. In fact, Jesus was aware they would.

Jesus models the opposite of what our church growth seminars are teaching us: How to lose disciples and drive away a large crowd. This isn't to say Jesus always did this. He welcomed crowds and called many disciples but Jesus also knew there were times to let people go.

As we ready ourselves to move onto the next section, we need to address the reality that sometimes it is the pastor/leader who needs to leave. When the toxicity and anxiousness begins to tear the pastor apart, the pastor needs to ask the Lord if it's time to move on. It may be the pastor who needs to exit to maintain mental and physical health.

GRACE AND TRUTH

Since we aren't Jesus and we do sin, we need to acknowledge two more things after going through this journey of how Jesus ministered to anxious people. First, we need to understand that Jesus always operated in the way of love. He was completely and utterly loving to every person he came in contact with. He loves each person fully as an image-bearer. Even when he confronted religious leaders or sin in others, it was always with complete love. In the Gospel of John, He is described as being full of grace and truth.[8] When we minister to people we have a tendency to oscillate between grace and truth. We have a tendency to favor, depending on the circumstance, either grace or truth. This makes it hard for us to do the other thing that Jesus did fully and completely: Staying on mission. He was not double-minded about the things he did nor the way he ministered. He was consistently the same in every circumstance.

I bring up these two concepts, grace and truth, before we dive into my final three thoughts of pastoring people because we need to see these as goals. At the same time, we also need to be ready to embrace grace for ourselves as we waffle or act double-minded. We can head towards consistency and resilience, but we will come up short and this is why we need Jesus, and we need others.

---

8. John 1:14

THREE FINAL THOUGHTS

1. The Leadership Sharing Approach

One of the best ways to pastor anxious people is to not do it all by yourself. You shouldn't be responsible for everyone. It's not realistic and it's not ideal. It's also impossible to make wise and healthy decisions at a high level of consistency. Once Jesus ascended into heaven, the model of leadership became councils, teams, pairs, elders, and partnerships. The early church realized that to lead best was to do it together. No individual was going to replace Jesus because He can't be replaced, shouldn't be replaced, and didn't need to be replaced as He promised to stay with us. Yet many pastors and leaders act like the best approach to leadership is to have "everything go through me."

Having a team does a variety of amazing things for your church. First, it multiplies the non-anxious leadership which allows more and more people to catch this way of being the body of Christ. Second, it creates opportunities for things to be thought through in deep and creative ways. This gives ideas the best chance to succeed. Third, it shares the responsibility of the decision. I don't know how many times I have been able to blame the leadership team for a decision that someone didn't like. Not to say I wasn't involved in the decision, but to say, "The leadership team decided _____." This makes it requisite that the person's complaint either has to be dropped or they could come and appeal before the whole team of people. Typically, they don't want to do that. If the issue does go to the leadership team, the decision is made as a group and allows for the fourth amazing thing a team does for your church; it shares the burden of leadership. It's hard for anxiousness to spread when there is a team of people working actively against it.

2. Saying Sorry

I'm sorry it took me so long to get to this point since it's so very important. In fact, it may be a tangible evidence of your non-anxious pastoring. To apologize is humbling and helpful. There will be times when you and/or your team doesn't make the right call. If you can learn to say "I'm sorry," this helps the anxiousness in the church stay under control. Now you may be thinking, *But what if they see you as a weak leader because you said you're sorry and that makes them more anxious.* I think being a humble leader is one hundred times better than being a strong leader. The majority of people would love to hear you say sorry more often and won't think less of you. They *will* think less of you when it's obvious you messed up and then refuse to apologize. Say sorry early and often.

3. Creating Trust

I once had a lady in my congregation tell me bluntly that I wasn't her pastor yet. This took me aback since she had been attending our church for a few months and she typically remarked on how the sermons had helped her tremendously. I asked her what she meant, and she told me that she wasn't sure she could trust me yet. There were many pastors that she had trusted in the past, and they broke her trust in one way or another. She expressed that she was okay with sitting under my preaching and coming to the church, but she wasn't ready yet to call me her pastor. I truly wanted to be offended. The ego in me probably was, but I felt the Holy Spirit remind me that He was working in this woman and that my whole role was to be a pastor worthy of her trust. This is a very important key to pastoring anxious people. You have to create trust or people (anxious or otherwise) won't let you pastor them. They may not be as blunt as the lady in my story, but they may still have the same idea in their heads; *You can preach to me but you can't pastor me.* If you truly want to pastor anxious people, be a person they can trust with their anxiousness.

Chapter 10

Becoming a Non-Anxious Church

I DREAM OF A new version of church, not just at the local church I get to pastor but an entirely new church culture: one in which pastors aren't bullied nor do they become the bully; church that doesn't make new people feel anxious or church kids grow up feeling exhausted; an environment that doesn't produce performances but disciples; where pastor's kids don't lose their parents every weeknight and weekend to "the work of the Lord and building the church."

If the goal for the church has been to make disciples, we have turned it into a machine-like factory. We have valued production more than quality and so we have factory-produced Christians. They may look the part, often even do the part, but their inner life is a mess. Their discipleship looks like idolatry and the church becomes something to consume instead of a family to belong to. If we focus solely on the number of disciples, this allows us to produce "disciples" at a higher, cheaper, and faster rate. We cheapen discipleship by making it a production instead of a journey. We create programs to change people without inviting the Holy Spirit to move. We often care more about how many people sign up instead of how many people grow up.

Why do we keep doing it? For the same reason I bought a toy for my four-year-old son last Christmas. It was a very specific toy he wanted and sure enough, there was only one maker and one supplier. Many of the reviews for this toy said something to the effect of, "Don't buy this toy. It's cheaply made and breaks in the first few minutes." This didn't seem promising. However, it wasn't very expensive (so no big waste right?), it was almost Christmas, it was easy to order, and it was the exact toy he wanted with no other options. We bought it and sure enough, it broke within the first few minutes.

We make these same decisions with discipleship. It's not going to cost us a lot, seems pretty easy to make happen and there are people demanding discipleship from us; (congregants, denominational leaders, or hopefully our own desire to bring discipleship to our people). It feels like there's a deadline, the parishioners are saying it's what they want, and what other options do we have? We keep buying it and continue to regret it. It's almost like a cheaply made toy that's predictably disposable or dysfunctional. When we produce disciples in the same factory we will find the same results.

If we want to become a non-anxious church we will need new answers to making disciples. Or maybe better stated, ancient answers. Throughout this book, I've shared a lot about becoming a non-anxious church but now we need to put a plan in place. Whether you are a congregant, volunteer, pastor, or denominational leader, you all have a role to play.

As we close this book and set a plan in place, we need to look at the two final things getting in the way of becoming a non-anxious church. We have just touched on both of these, but let's dig into them in more detail. First, we have essentially fast-tracked discipleship, and second, we have defined success by our own metrics instead of kingdom metrics. I'll offer solutions to these two problems later in this chapter. If we can embrace these solutions and then create a realistic plan for our church and for ourselves, we can join the movement of churches seeking the non-anxious way.

Before we get to those, I want to encourage you from the example of King Asa in 2 Chronicles 15. Our path forward will look a lot like his in this journey out of "anxious church" to "non-anxious church." The first seven verses essentially correlate to the first seven chapters of this book. Read them and see what you notice:

> The Spirit of God came on Azariah son of Oded. He went out to meet Asa and said to him, "Listen to me, Asa and all Judah and Benjamin. The Lord is with you when you are with him. If you seek him, he will be found by you, but if you forsake him, he will forsake you. For a long time Israel was without the true God, without a priest to teach and without the law. But in their distress they turned to the Lord, the God of Israel, and sought him, and he was found by them. In those days it was not safe to travel about, for all the inhabitants of the lands were in great turmoil. One nation was being crushed by another and one city by another, because God

was troubling them with every kind of distress. But as for you, be strong and do not give up, for your work will be rewarded."

The prophet Azariah comes to King Asa who is the leader of the land and God's people. He reminds him of his important responsibility with such leadership. A few lines stick out to me.

In verse 2, we see this promise and its condition, "The Lord is with you when you are with him." Generations later, Jesus gave the same assurance with a charge in John 15:4; "Remain in me, as I also remain in you." This is the essential task of a disciple of Jesus and even more so of a leader of people, because the health of a church correlates directly to the health of the leaders. Prophet Azariah also says in verse 2; "If you seek him, he will be found by you." Once again these are words we find in Jesus' mouth, "But seek first his kingdom and his righteousness, and all these things will be given to you as well."[1] What are "all these things"? The things you are worried about. How do you combat anxiousness and worry in Jesus' mind? Seeking the kingdom of God. Prophet Azariah says to King Asa, *if you want to lead the way God wants you to lead, seek God and you will find him.* The above statement is backed up with the flipside of not seeking God: "But if you forsake him, he will forsake you." The warning is that if you decide to walk in a way where God is not leading, he isn't going to force you on the right path. You get to decide if you want to follow God or follow other ways. A church that forsakes or abandons the way of God may look right and sound right, but grievously doesn't have the Spirit of God convicting, empowering, and sanctifying the body.

We see in verses 5 and 6 that there are many disturbances and distresses, but the goal of King Asa's leadership is to "Be strong and do not give up, for your work will be rewarded." The work the church has been called to is important but you will need to be strong, and please don't give up. If you help people seek God and find the kingdom, the reward is great.

King Asa heard these words and began to act on them. *If the Lord is with me when I am with Him, then I need to be* with *Him.* There are four leadership postures and programs that King Asa began to implement immediately. Verse 8 tells us the first three things he did: "When Asa heard these words and the prophecy of Azariah son of Oded the prophet, he took courage. He removed the detestable idols from the whole land of Judah and Benjamin and from the towns he had captured in the hills of Ephraim. He

---

1. Matthew 6:33

repaired the altar of the Lord that was in front of the portico of the Lord's temple."

The first thing he had to do was muster up the courage to make this a reality. The same is true for us if we are going to become a non-anxious church. We need to take courage because anxiousness is going to hate your non-anxiousness. Opposition will arise almost immediately and you need to know the Lord your God is with you in this endeavor. Satan's job description from John 10:10 is to "steal, kill, and destroy." He won't make it easy to lead and to lead well.

TAKE COURAGE

Is this even possible? If we don't embrace anxiousness, how will we succeed? What about all the people pushing towards production and "progress"? How will we keep up with the other churches in our denomination and area? Am I even the right leader to help make this a reality? What if people leave? What if staff doesn't buy in? Fear plagues us, beats us down, lies to us, tells us we aren't enough, convinces us we can't do it. We are tempted to turn back and go back to what was comfortable and normal for us. If you are living in a place of fear as you embrace this journey, take courage because God is with you. Fear wants to discourage you and blind you to the "God with us" life. Remember the amazing promise from Azariah; God is with you if you desire to be with Him. This is a great assurance and therefore there is no need to fear.

The second thing we see King Asa set out to do is to remove idols: "He took courage and removed the detestable idols from the whole land of Judah and Benjamin . . . "

REMOVE IDOLS

This is where not fearing plays a big role. Removing idols in your life is hard enough. Try removing idols in the church culture. There will be backlash. People will even think you have lost sight of the gospel, since their discipleship has been tied with idolatry. It is important to identify the idols that are in your church and in your own ministry. What are those idols? Is it success, pride, politics, money? As I am sure you are aware, idolatry is anything that demands your worship, attention, life, and sacrifice. Some of these things may not seem like idols because they are ingrained in the way we do and think about church. We remember that Martha wasn't even aware that she was anxious or lost in her production to miss sitting at the feet of Jesus.

Here are questions to consider while you examine the next steps in becoming a non-anxious church:

- What keeps your leadership, congregants, and staff from sitting at the feet of Jesus?
- What blocks your church's view of God?
- Where does your church's time/love/money/attention/sacrifice go? Is it the same places Jesus would put his energy, attention, time, and money?
- What makes your church act anxious? What would it look like to remove those idols?

We need to remove any idols in our way of being with Jesus. If you are struggling to identify them, ask God to reveal them, so as a church you can remove them. After he removed the idols and really probably while he was removing the idols, 2 Chronicles 15:8 says, "He repaired the altar of the Lord that was in front of the portico of the Lord's temple."

REPAIR THE ALTAR OF THE LORD

King Asa knew that it's not simply removing something that suddenly fixes all the issues. There needs to be a replacing of what was taken away with what is right. As humans, when we remove one bad habit, if we don't replace it with a good habit, typically a new bad habit steps in and takes its place. Since humans are created to worship, we all do it in one way or another. If we remove our unhealthy worship and don't replace it with rightful worship, we will find a new thing for unhealthy worship. We will build and find a new idol. When we need to "repair the altar of the Lord," we are headed back to what we were designed for. We were designed to be with God and to be like God. For these purposes, I direct you back to chapter 6 to begin to build in habits that increase the growth of these ten postures of a non-anxious church. It's the next verses in the description of King Asa's ministry that really determined whether this strategy would live or die. 2 Chronicles 15:9–15 says:

Then he assembled all Judah and Benjamin and the people from Ephraim, Manasseh and Simeon who had settled among them, for large numbers had come over to him from Israel when they saw that the Lord his God was with him. They assembled at Jerusalem in the third month of the fifteenth year of Asa's reign. At that time they sacrificed to the Lord seven hundred head of cattle and seven thousand sheep and goats from the plunder they had brought back. They entered into a covenant to seek the Lord, the God of their ancestors, with all their heart and soul. All who would not seek the Lord, the God of Israel, were to be put to death, whether small or great, man or woman. They took an oath to the Lord with loud acclamation, with shouting and with trumpets and horns. All Judah rejoiced about the oath because they had sworn it wholeheartedly. They sought God eagerly, and he was found by them. So the Lord gave them rest on every side.

ASSEMBLE THE CONGREGATION AND CHALLENGE THEM

King Asa went through the steps of taking courage, removing idols, and repairing the altar to the Lord, he then gathers his people together and challenges them to be part of this endeavor. We need to do this from the beginning of our journey towards non-anxious churches. Don't do this alone. If you are the only non-anxious leader in your church, your first step is to begin to disciple and recruit more non-anxious leaders. A solo non-anxious leader who begins to tear down idols and repair altars will eventually no longer be the leader. Anxiousness will rally the people and they'll remove the leader that is destroying "all the things that matter." Now you can't threaten people with death like King Asa did but hopefully through intentional leadership and convicting preaching through the power of the Holy Spirit, people will want to join in this endeavor. Notice what they do in this passage:

- They sacrificed to the Lord.
- They entered into a covenant—to seek God with all their heart and soul (all together).
- They rejoiced.
- They sought God eagerly (wholeheartedly).

I don't want you to miss what happens next. After they did all these things that renewed their focus on the Lord, it says, "The Lord gave them rest on every side." When they pursued God, it didn't create a sense of go, go, go, or do, do, do, which is often how we envision what it looks like to follow God, but instead, they found the restful way. The one Jesus describes when he says, "Come to me, all you who are weary and burdened, and I will give you rest."[2]

I would be failing you if I didn't describe the next two verses in 2 Chronicles 15. Verses 16 and 17 say; "King Asa also deposed his grandmother Maakah from her position as queen mother, because she had made a repulsive image for the worship of Asherah. Asa cut it down, broke it up, and burned it in the Kidron Valley. Although he did not remove the high places from Israel, Asa's heart was fully committed to the Lord all his life." Notice a couple of important things. He had to remove a very prominent member of leadership in the land. Awkward enough for him, they were related. We may also have to remove some influence towards anxiousness and this is going to be hard, frustrating, and even sad. We also see in verse 17 that he wasn't able to remove all the idols and there were still a few that remained, but it wasn't because of King Asa. His "heart was fully committed to the Lord all his life." There may be some churches and ministries where the long and slow way of removing things may not happen under your ministry but you were able to stay personally devoted to the Lord and do what you are able.

Therefore non-anxious leaders, take courage, you can and you must remove the idols. You can and you must go back to the original design! And you must challenge others to do the same, but you are not alone, and you can't do this alone. Do it in the power of Christ through the Holy Spirit with the help of other non-anxious leaders.

Let's take a look now at the way towards slow discipleship and redefining success. These are the answers for our struggles with fast-tracking discipleship and measuring our success based on metrics that aren't kingdom metrics.

SLOW DISCIPLESHIP

We have spent a lot of the book expounding on this topic. Mary of Bethany sits at the feet of Jesus, learning and abiding. This posture isn't fast. You can't

2. Matthew 11:28

put Jesus on 2x speed like you can an audiobook. You have to learn at the pace he teaches and the pace you can retain and learn.

As I continue to remind you, we need to remember that list of ten postures a non-anxious church will embody from chapter 6. Those don't come from fast-tracking discipleship. Therefore, there is going to be work to do: obedient work, slow work, hard work. I love what author and pastor John Mark Comer says about this concept: "There's no killer app for the soul; souls are grown the ancient way, like trees, slowly, over decades, on a timescale entirely different to that of human civilization, by sinking roots deep and waiting patiently."[3]

The reality of good discipleship is that it's slow and works best over different seasons, circumstances, and opportunities. Humans need to grow in the good times and the bad; see God working on the mountaintop, and see his hand moving in the valley. We need to learn how to make it through long hard winters and how to trust God when we relax with a cold drink on a warm summer day. The Bible actually says that one of the best discipleship strategies is one that absolutely zero churches are embracing intentionally: suffering. James 1:2–12 says:

> Consider it pure joy, my brothers and sisters, whenever you face trials of many kinds, because you know that the testing of your faith produces perseverance. Let perseverance finish its work so that you may be mature and complete, not lacking anything. If any of you lacks wisdom, you should ask God, who gives generously to all without finding fault, and it will be given to you. But when you ask, you must believe and not doubt, because the one who doubts is like a wave of the sea, blown and tossed by the wind. That person should not expect to receive anything from the Lord. Such a person is double-minded and unstable in all they do.
>
> Believers in humble circumstances ought to take pride in their high position. But the rich should take pride in their humiliation—since they will pass away like a wildflower. For the sun rises with scorching heat and withers the plant; its blossom falls and its beauty is destroyed. In the same way, the rich will fade away even while they go about their business. Blessed is the one who perseveres under trial because, having stood the test, that person will receive the crown of life that the Lord has promised to those who love him.

---

3. Comer, *Different, Harder, Longer, Better,* 07/25

James gives us one long recipe for life-long discipleship here: Testing produces perseverance, perseverance matures which helps you be content and this actually brings about wisdom. This wisdom anchors us so as to not be double-minded. Doubt that produces double-mindedness is no longer a fruit of this believer's life. Interestingly enough, there probably aren't many people that you and I can think of who can say, "Yup, that's me!" Why is that? Because the way of the western Christian is not to let testing produce perseverance. We find the fastest way out of testing and we are unable to be resilient. I would assume if you are a leader or a pastor, this passage even makes you nervous. You think that the Christians in your church, with too much testing, may actually walk away from Jesus, not towards him. Isn't this a big red flag to our discipleship models?

Let me use an analogy here straight from the text. The greek word here for testing is "dokimion." This word is important because the usage of this word is the same as in other passages talking about the process of refining silver or gold. This is actually how James wants us to see this word here. It's not a test that's "let's see if your faith is real or not," but instead, it's a way of making your faith more "pure" as you would with gold or silver. The image is of putting the metal rod in the fire to make a blade. The idea is to heat up impure gold or silver to remove any impurities as the fire will melt them away. The hard part with these forges is that they get so hot, it takes a great deal of patience to leave the metal or the gold in the fire.

Tod Bolsinger in his book *Tempered Resilience* talks about the best leaders being those who have learned the art of the forge.[4] According to him, to be a tempered leader is to know what it looks like to be formed in leading, forged in self-reflection, learning relational security, using the stress of life to become a better leader, finding resilience in practice, and finding the rhythm of leading and not leading. He uses the forge as an example the whole way through. It is really a great book for any leader. Here is a personal experience that stuck out to me: At one point, he attended a class where he learned the art of the forge. He said his instructor had them stick the metal rod in the fire and after a while pull it out to look at it. The instructor told them, "it may look cool, but it's 700 degrees and can burn the skin off your hands ... when a piece of steel looks like this, even coming out of the forge, it's not ready for shaping, if you hammer on it now, you'll only mar and scar it. And because it doesn't look any different, it's actually more dangerous. If we are going to make this steel into something that can

---

4. Bolsinger, *Tempered Resilience*.

be used, it needs to be much, much hotter—nearly 2,000 degrees. It has to be soft enough and malleable enough to take the shaping. And that requires a lot more heat. So, back into the fire it goes."[5]

Bolsinger goes on to tell his readers that you'll be tempted to think that you are ready when it's 700 degrees, but you have to resist. There is so much more heat to be added before you are really ready to be a change agent. It takes a great deal of patience with our people and with ourselves to let God work in the heat and the trials. If we can do this, we not only will have healthy people in our church but also become a healthier leader. We tend to want to jump in front of God and "do what we think God would do here." Often God may simply allow things to play out and we need patience in the process. The impurities, these idols we cling to, the complaints and frustrations of life, are diminished in the refining fire of Jesus. We have to learn to only depend and trust in him.

If we want to be a non-anxious church, we need to learn resilience, and resilience comes from slow discipleship. Resilience is something we need in a culture that is ever-changing, and anxiousness that is always wanting to suck us in. We have to stay strong and hold to the anchor. Bolsinger writes, "Resilience is not something that can be mustered in a moment of 'rising to the occasion.' It is formed over a long period *before* the crisis of testing so that it can continue the transformation *during* the moment of challenge" (Bolsinger's emphasis).[6]

Every single person will have trials and tests in their life. We don't manufacture them. We nurture our people within them. As a church, we get to be with people along their journey. We are there when someone loses a job. We are there when someone gets a new job, when a baby is born and an older saint dies, when someone has surgery and when that same person recovers. We get to be there when a new family comes to the church and when a beloved couple moves away. Slow discipleship is grateful for all these opportunities; grateful for the mountaintops and valley lows and recognizing that there are people in your church who are having those experiences simultaneously. When we see our people as growing along the journey, not only can we speak life into those moments, we can even join them in the midst of those moments. If we try to manufacture the growth we may actually derail the process.

---

5. Bolsinger, *Tempered Resilience*, 78–81.
6. Bolsinger, *Tempered Resilience*, 30.

Slow discipleship also recognizes God in all of life. Cameron McAllister and his dad, Stewart encourage families to recognize God's movement in their homes. They speak to this in their book, *Faith That Lasts*: "Encountering God and expecting him in the everyday is vital to forming our lives in Christ. If we never speak practically of God's presence, if we never seek him or consult him in our homes, we are communicating that God is only in the church or in so-called sacred spaces but largely absent in the living room, the bedroom, and the kitchen. We can unconsciously teach the family a form of functional atheism or a form of deism—the idea that God is a distant technician who set creation in motion and now remains uninterested in the daily circumstances of our lives."[7]

I love to tell our church that the same God who is with you in your trial is the same God who is with you when you are brushing your teeth. The God of the Thanksgiving feast is the God of the thrown-together breakfast. He is with us on our mountaintops, valleys, but also on the mundane paths in between. This is exactly what discipleship looks like; learning to be with Jesus and like Jesus in all aspects of life. God isn't meant to be shelved during the week and dusted off on Sundays. For the Christian, it is Christ in you—always. If we can teach this as a church we become much less anxious about our people, our programs, and our Sunday gatherings. We don't have to put so much pressure on "one thing" or "one event." We can trust that Jesus, the Good Shepherd, is shepherding them in all things and through all things.

What does slow discipleship mean for a church? Three of the important things are these:

- Faithfulness. It's committing to the long and steady way, not the quick and easy decisions.
- Don't give people easy outs. It's so easy for a church to see a person who is working through something and instead of helping them work through it, we give them an easy "out." Instead of discernment, we give them the answer. It's similar to helping your child do a math worksheet but after the third problem being frustrated with the teaching process and finding it much easier to simply tell them the answers. This doesn't help them learn. This helps them regurgitate answers. Instead of telling our people what to do or how to do it, what if we teach them the process of discerning the way of faith? If we are okay

[7]. McAllister and McAllister, *Faith That Lasts*, 108.

with pastoring people *in* process we can be less anxious about where people *are* in the process.
- Help people learn the reality of God in all of life.

I feel like I need to say one more thing. I don't want to pendulum swing here. Slow discipleship doesn't mean a church won't and shouldn't do fun things or plan outreach events. I would argue it actually means the opposite. However, the focus is on a more healthy trajectory. Instead of planning outreach events because we "need more people" or "it makes us look good," we do it because it helps people outside the church step into and follow along the discipleship journey. We should also plan events and activities that are fun. Simply because they are fun. There is so much joy that comes from God when his people gather to laugh and enjoy each other. The non-anxious church will actually do outreach and events better than the anxious church because success is defined in a non-anxious way.

This leads us to our next step in becoming a non-anxious church. This one may even be our most important step because everything else will hang on the back of what we define as "success."

REDEFINE SUCCESS

I noticed that a new family had been attending our church for a few months, a young mom with her two little kids. This is a trendy-looking mom with adorable children. One week we got to talking after church and she said something that caught me off guard. She observed, "This church is not a very cool church." I think she could see I was startled by such a bold statement and she continued, "I mean, that's good. My husband loves God but he has been burned by churches. He hasn't wanted to come with me because he isn't ready for another 'cool' church. He needs a place where he can come and be himself."

I wasn't surprised by the reality that we weren't a "cool" church. We clearly weren't and still aren't nor are we trying to be a "cool" church. That's not how we define success. However, this young mom brings up a very pertinent assessment of the current state of churches. There are many churches working hard to present themselves as cool, trendy, and successful, which doesn't leave much room for authentic, relatable, and Christ-like. Do I think there are a bunch of churches out there intentionally defining success as being a cool church? Probably not, but in the social media era we always try to present our best selves and leave the rest hidden away. We want to be seen as cool and so we work to project that image.

It's really as simple as the concept of "you are what you eat" or "you become what you behold." These expressions convey the truth that what you put into yourself, or what you fix your attention on truly matters. This is not only true for the individual Christian but it's overwhelmingly true for the living organism of the church. The life of the church is going to head in the direction of where it put its greatest attention.

My theory is that the most anxious churches will have such a spattering of "defined successes" that it's even what's driving the anxiousness. So many desires are pushing for attention, all the things the church is told to be and to look like. "Cool" is just one of a long list of things people look for in a church.

This would also explain why church growth books are some of the highest-selling books. Churches are lost in anxiousness and are hoping someone with more "success" will tell them how to be "successful." The desires of the church are pulling in so many directions towards completely different definitions of success.

I'm reminded of a Charles Spurgeon quote from a sermon titled, "The Anxious Inquirer." He is speaking about the seeker being drawn in by God, but it's easy to see the correlation to the church seeking so many things and also being drawn in by God. "It is a blessed thing for a man when he has brought his desires into a focus. When a man has fifty different desires, his heart resembles a pool of water, which is spread over a marsh, breeding miasma and pestilence; but when all his desires are brought into one channel, his heart becomes like a river of pure water, running along and fertilizing the fields. Happy is the man who hath one desire, if that one desire is set on Christ, though it may not yet have been realized. If it be his desire, it is a blessed sign of the divine work within him."[8]

How does a church caught up in chasing many versions of success find the path forward? First, let's answer the question: How do most churches currently define success? The main ways? Attendance and Money. There are many subcategories too and we already mentioned "cool," but we could throw in "activism" or "conservative" as more examples. Really, it's any way that congregants, staff, leadership, even the denomination would define success. Think back to all the demands that come at a pastor in chapter 2.

---

8. Spurgeon, "The Anxious Inquirer."

These are ways in which a pastor not only tries to stay afloat, but if he does them well, he "succeeds!"

Spurgeon said the person with fifty desires is like a stinky bug-infested marshland. This is the outflow of an anxious church. It's chasing after the still waters but making them stagnant.

We've already identified the two ingredients that the majority of the desires stem from. Congregations with more people and more money are considered "successful." Even if people don't say it with their mouth, they secretly think it in their mind. A church that is succeeding in these two areas won't be touched until the stinky marsh begins to turn up disease. Everyone wanted to be like that church and secretly still does (just not the part that got them in trouble). If we have defined success in such a way, then we will become what we behold. The "becoming" doesn't mean more people and more money. This typically doesn't happen from beholding these churches as models. Instead, we get the stinky marsh. The church that beholds these as "success" gets the anxiety of chasing it down.

Consequently, we need to define success differently and ask better questions. Jesus told Martha it's the one thing. Spurgeon said it's narrowing it all the way down to one desire. The Apostle Paul says we are being transformed by staring down God's glory,[9] becoming what we behold. If what we are beholding is God's glory, then we are being transformed by it. This is the key.

My siblings and I were all born in Tennessee, though we moved to the west coast when we were children. My sister was the oldest at ten years old when we left. Ten years is long enough for the south to be buried deep in one's soul. In my sister, down in the depths, there is a southern girl and we get to see it come out every time another southerner is around. If she has even a five-minute conversation with someone from the deep south with their thick accent, she will walk away speaking with a similar accent and not even realize it. My brother and I love to tease her about this—"Why are you talking that way?"

What we see in action is that she is being transformed by what she is focused on, things around her and things within her. This is the journey of a Christian too. If you believe in Jesus and follow his way, he has left his Spirit within you. The Holy Spirit is there down in the depths of your soul and the goal is to give the Spirit the ability to transform you by beholding God's glory. How do you do this? By spending time with Jesus through

---

9. 2 Corinthians 3:18

his Word and in many other spiritual disciplines. How does a church do this? How do we become what we behold? The same way. Behind closed doors, we need to stop beholding the marketing strategies and desires of a celebrity pastor. The Spirit needs access in our budget meetings, our staff get-togethers, and our worship practices, etc. It sounds silly to say all this, but we are being transformed by something. If we are steadfastly beholding more attendance and money, that will change the culture of our church. If we are devotedly beholding the glory of God, that will also change our church. Who do we want to become as a church?

How do we do this? It sounds so spiritual and not enough like boots on the ground. It starts by asking better questions. Can we define success without using money and attendance? What are some of the other things we define as success? Why? What would it look like to change the definition, and how do we measure *those* things? Some things may not be measurable and that's important. We've explored this throughout the book, but it's important to see again that Jesus didn't define success with metrics most churches use today (attendance, giving, building size). The crowds would come and that was good, but the crowds would leave and it was also considered good. He was fine with a crowd of one or a crowd of many. We can surmise that attendance wasn't a metric he used to define success in the kingdom of God. He also didn't define it by his budget. The first indicator of this is that his financial secretary was a thief, dipping into the offerings. Second, he never gives us a breakdown on how to successfully raise money and there is no chapter on capital campaigns. It was a secondary (maybe even tertiary or quaternary) thought, but not primary in the kingdom of God.

However, Jesus didn't throw these two things out with the bathwater either. Let's be careful not to overcorrect and pretend that these metrics don't matter at all. It would be so easy for us to say that these things make us anxious and so we shouldn't track them or care about them at all. However, this would be a major error. Actually, Jesus and his disciples did take these things into account but, once again, it wasn't primary. They knew often how many people were in the crowd, thus someone was taking attendance. They also had a financial secretary in Judas and John knew he was dipping into the bag and stealing, so they were tracking how much was supposed to be in there.

To monitor these concerns doesn't make an anxious church but this anxiousness comes from focusing on them as of primary importance and measuring your church's worth based on such things. If attendance is up, the pastor feels more worthwhile. If it's down, they feel inadequate. If the budget is being met, the church applauds the pastor. If the budget is short, the pastor needs to do more to increase the budget. This is the anxious cycle because when the focus becomes primary, it actually makes it harder to get out of the cycle. If this becomes the case, the blinders get put on to anything and everything else. To go back to Spurgeon's illustration, the swamp is moving more fetid water into the pool.

The focus needs to shift to Jesus and Jesus alone. The Jesus of the highs, the lows, and everything in between. Jesus is guiding and building his church through the faithful commitment of the community of believers to each other and to the kingdom of God. Once again, this doesn't mean we should do things in a way that isn't good, engaging, or well-thought-out. No one would accuse Jesus of not being good or engaging. Pastors don't use focus on Jesus as an excuse to be neglectful or lazy in their vocation. Continue to behold the glory of the Lord and be transformed by it, and the Sanctifier will help you grow in your gifts and calling.

ACTION PLAN

This seems like a good point to transition to our final objective of becoming a non-anxious church. An action plan is called for, whether you are a congregant, leader, pastor, or denominational leader. What do the next steps look like?

My advice is to step into Dallas Willard's VIM model[10] to help begin and navigate this journey. Let's use weight loss as an example to understand this model and then transition it into the non-anxious church action plan. The "V" stands for vision. The first step is to imagine and envision what it looks like to be at your ideal weight. Maybe you imagine how you will feel, what you will look like, what outfit you want to wear. This is step one. If you leave it here though, you will not lose even one pound of weight. Yet, we don't want to skip this step. We have to keep the vision in front of us as it reminds us of our target and our dream. The "I" stands for intention. This is when you begin to plan and take steps to put the weight loss in motion. You go and buy that outfit in your ideal size. You research workout plans, you sign up for a gym, you get a trainer or a workout partner. Once again though, if you stop here you will lose zero pounds. But just like "V" you can't skip this step. One of the most common ways a plan fails is to jump

10. Willard, *Renovation of the Heart*, 85.

into "M" before taking the steps for it. If you were to say, *Tomorrow I will wake up and lose 25 pounds,* and you don't buy the running shoes or map the route or come up with a great schedule, you will quit almost as quickly as you started. Intention helps you create sustainability with a plan.

The "M" stands for means. Means is what happens when you work out, when you run, when you lift the weights or jog around the track. It's actually putting the vision and intentions in motion. If we return to our example of King Ahab at the beginning of the chapter we can see the "VIM" model in motion. King Ahab was stirred by the "vision" of bringing his kingdom back to worshipping Yahweh and Yahweh only. The "intentions" were first taking courage, tearing down the idols, and repairing the altar of the Lord. He finally put his last intention in motion by challenging the congregation to worship Yahweh and only Yahweh. The "means" was when the king and the people actually did worship Yahweh earnestly and with all their heart.

To become a non-anxious church, you will need to take up the same idea. No matter what position of authority or non-authority you have in your church, you can't just say "we will be a non-anxious church," wave the magic wand and presto—non-anxious church! It won't work. You install the vision for what that looks like, you create the plan to see it through, and then you actually see it through and accomplish your goal.

This will obviously look different for the congregant than it will for the pastor or the chair of the church. This will look different for the volunteer usher than it will for the associate pastor. To be a truly non-anxious church though, everyone needs to be committed to it. All hands on deck. If the leadership of the church has taken up the call to make this a reality, they will have to do a lot of self-examination to see how far the changes need to go and how deep the anxiousness runs. There will be some churches that can repair the altar and things begin to click. There will be others that will have to remove many, many idols. The spectrum of becoming a non-anxious church could range from simply changing the leadership style on one end to complete deconstruction on the other. It has to start somewhere and with someone. I pray that someone is you.

Years ago there was a viral Ted Talk from Derek Sivers that has 1.4 million views on YouTube as of this writing. He titled his talk, "How to Start a Movement."[11] It is delightful and hilarious as he demonstrates how leadership works using a random dancer at a music festival. This lone guy

---

11. Sivers, "How to Start a Movement."

is dancing his heart out all by himself. It's something most of us would chuckle to ourselves about while remarking how embarrassing that would be if we were him. Then something remarkable happens; another dancer joins him. Now it is two guys dancing together and this second guy turns and gestures to a couple of friends off the screen to join them. Soon there is a small group dancing together. It's this small group that begins the movement because before the video ends and Sivers completes his Ted Talk, the entire screen is full of dancers. It was officially a movement.

We can learn a lot about becoming a non-anxious church from this lone dancer. He wasn't doing it to start a movement. In fact, he seemed a little startled when it started to gain traction. He was simply living and dancing without concern. You could call him a non-anxious dancer. The movement started with one person who was committed to the dance. The non-anxious church starts with one person committed to becoming a non-anxious person. When we see the second person join the lone dancer, Sivers calls this person the "first follower." He says that this is the most essential position for the creation of a movement. He smiles as he says, "the first follower is what transforms a lone nut into a leader."[12] The first follower notices the lone dancer and thinks, *That's it! That's what I need to be doing. That looks like the perfect way to enjoy this music. I must dance!* The lone dancer has inspired a second dancer and now there are two.

The non-anxious person attracts others who also want to become non-anxious people. This first follower also calls others into the dance. This is when a small group of people begin to make a change to the hillside. This hillside, which consisted mostly of people consuming a music festival, now has a growing movement of participants in the music. No longer content to watch absentmindedly, they are now throwing themselves into the music and creating a new culture. The non-anxious small group begins to change the culture.

This is your journey ahead if you choose to start a movement of dancers on a hillside:

1. Dance.
2. Watch for others to come.
3. Teach them to dance.
4. Invite others to dance.

12. Sivers, "How To Start a Movement."

5. Change the culture.

To spell it out in more clear terms for the purposes of becoming a non-anxious church:

1. Work on becoming a non-anxious person (sit at the feet of Jesus).
2. God will draw others toward you.
3. Walk with them towards becoming non-anxious people and leaders.
4. Invite more to embrace this non-anxious way.
5. Watch as the culture changes (especially as more and more non-anxious people fill leadership roles).

Doesn't seem so out of reach now does it? Let me ask you before we close: What does it look like for you to be part of this process? Let's take steps together. As we saw in chapter 1, we serve a God who not only is calling us to this in peace and order but he is helping us in the journey. He sanctifies and He empowers. Find refuge in Him, and only in Him, and He will lead you through this process. Begin today; begin now to write out some thoughts, pray through them, rally other leaders to them, and take steps in that direction.

Epilogue

"Grace is the first and last word of the Christian life, and all of us are desperately in need of mercy and are deeply loved."[1]

—Tish Harrison Warren

I HAVE A CONFESSION to make. It has taken the entire book for me to own up to the reality that I am not a non-anxious pastor, nor is the church where I pastor a non-anxious church. Yet, we aspire to be. I also work towards this direction and long to be Mary at the feet of Jesus.

Early on in the process of writing this book, I was sharing it with others to provide feedback. A question I received early on was; "Do you believe there are any non-anxious pastors or non-anxious churches?" My initial reaction was to say, "Somewhere, hopefully." With more reflection, I think no church nor pastor would identify themselves fully there. The closer we get to Jesus, the more clearly we see our own need for him. So then, as we grow as a church we will only see more of our need for sitting at the feet of Jesus.

Dallas Willard wrote in a couple of his books that he thinks the church has much to learn from a 12-step group. He wrote in the endnotes of *The Divine Conspiracy*, "One sees how utterly superficial the consumer Christianity of our day is. Imagine, by contrast, being a member of a Church or local assembly of Christians where these 12 steps were applied without specific reference to alcohol."[2] He goes further down this track when he writes in the *Renovation of the Heart*: "Historically, the AA program was closely aligned with the church and Christian traditions, and now it has much to

---

1. Warren, *Prayer in the Night*, 8.
2. Willard, *The Divine Conspiracy*, 416.

give back to a church that has largely lost its grip on spiritual formation as a standard path of Christian life. Any successful plan for spiritual formation, whether for the individual or group, will in fact be significantly similar to the Alcoholics Anonymous program."[3]

Why does he think that the church can learn from AA groups? While all twelve steps can help us grow, it all hinges on the first two steps: "Admitting we are powerless" and "knowing there is a power greater than us (God) who can restore us."[4] Imagine if we all came with this sort of humility to church; as congregants and leaders knowing we are in desperate need of grace and growth; knowing we are powerless to do church on our own, in our own strength, and admitting we have tried many times.

What if we came to Jesus as Peter came to Jesus on the waves,[5] full of faith and yet full of failure. Peter walks on the waves with doubts that the waves will hold him; with doubts that this is even reality; with doubts that Jesus can be trusted with such things, and he begins to sink. The moral of the story is not that we shouldn't be like Peter, and if we get a shot to walk on water, we need to have zero doubts. The moral of the story is that Jesus "reached out his hand and caught him." Jesus is the savior, the rescuer, as he has always been and always will be. We will never walk on waves without any doubts. We will never pastor a church or participate in a church without any anxiousness. Instead of pushing Jesus' hand away, let him pull you up out of the waves. The goal is not to muscle your way up, to find some faith for what you can't do in your own strength; but instead to keep your eyes on Jesus and grab his hand when your eyes falter. This is grace and this is what runs a church.

This is what Charles Spurgeon is telling us at the end of the quote we used in the last chapter: "It is a blessed thing for a man when he has brought his desires into focus. When a man has fifty different desires, his heart resembles a pool of water, which is spread over a marsh, breeding miasma and pestilence; but when all his desires are brought into one channel, his heart becomes like a river of pure water, running along and fertilizing the fields. Happy is the man who hath one desire, if that one desire is set on Christ, though it may not yet have been realized. If it be his desire, it is a blessed sign of the divine work within him."[6]

3. Willard, *The Divine Conspiracy*, 416.
4. AA, "Alcoholics Anonymous 12 Steps."
5. Matthew 14:22–34
6. Spurgeon, "The Anxious Inquirer."

He says, "though it may not yet have been realized. If it be his desire, it is a blessed sign of the divine work within him." We get to the end of the book and need to find grace, not more "try-hard" churches because that's another whole level of anxiety. The non-anxious pastor and the non-anxious church may not yet be realized but it should be our desire. If it is your desire, God's already at work within you and within your church.

Anxiousness comes and goes because you are human but it's all about what you do with it; not that you have it or feel it. It's similar to the check-engine light of a car. When this light comes on it doesn't automatically mean the engine is failing. In fact, most often there is a smaller issue that needs to be addressed, as simple as replacing your gas cap to changing a spark plug; or it could be as big as a catalytic converter failure. The light is an indication that something needs to be addressed, not that the car has failed. Worry works in a similar way. When you feel worried about something, it is your body's way of saying *something needs to be looked at and addressed*. It could be as simple as taking deep breaths and moving along, or it could be big, like trauma coming to the surface.

When the check-engine light of a car comes on, you take it to the shop and the mechanic helps diagnose and fix the problem before it gets worse. When you feel worried you also need to take appropriate steps to diagnose the problem and find ways forward. There are trained professionals who can help with this, similar to the trained professionals that can help your car. The reality is, if you do nothing for either your car or yourself, it only gets worse. Even if you can go for years without addressing it, it's not going to work itself out.

How about when a church shows signs of anxiousness? The light has come on and if we don't do something about it, it will only grow worse. The anxious system will begin to produce the fruit it has been created to produce and our people and our pastors will suffer those results.

In this book, my goal was to turn on the check engine light for the pastor, leader, and the church, with the hope that the current and next generation of churches begin to embody the way of Jesus. The non-anxious way.

Appendix 1

Non-Anxious Church Quiz

How non-anxious would you say your church is right now? Below are the 10 marks of a non-anxious church from chapter 5. Each mark will have one or two questions that will allow you to rank your church on a scale of one to ten, based on how well you are doing with each practice. Ten is the best you could possibly be doing and one is acknowledging that as a church you are completely absent of the practice. Be honest, be kind, and be fair. There isn't a church out there that will get tens on every practice. If you score low, don't be hard on yourself or others, but instead commit to the hard work of becoming a non-anxious church.

After the quiz, let's study the results and work on a path forward towards a more non-anxious church.

1. **Non-anxious churches keep the focus in the right place.** Philippians 4:4.

Where does your church find its state of well-being? Is it in the Lord completely? (10)
Or is it in something else? (Attendance? Giving? Buildings? Community service? The Pastor?) (1)

$$| - 1 - 2 - 3 - 4 - 5 - 6 - 7 - 8 - 9 - 10 - |$$

Appendix 1

2. **Non-anxious churches are gentle and kind.** Philippians 4:5.

How would you rank your church's gentleness?

$$|-1-2-3-4-5-6-7-8-9-10-|$$

How would you rank your church's kindness?

$$|-1-2-3-4-5-6-7-8-9-10-|$$

3. **Non-anxious churches are prayerful.** Philippians 4:6a.

How much prayer happens at your church? Not just in church services but in small groups, leadership team meetings, staff meetings, committee meetings, etc.

$$|-1-2-3-4-5-6-7-8-9-10-|$$

4. **Non-anxious churches are thankful.** Philippians 4:6b.

Does your church exude thankfulness (10) or as a body do you come across as entitled, consumeristic, grumpy, bitter, etc. (1)?

$$|-1-2-3-4-5-6-7-8-9-10-|$$

Where would you rank your church on encouraging and equipping?

$$|-1-2-3-4-5-6-7-8-9-10-|$$

5. **Non-anxious churches make non-anxious decisions.** Philippians 4:6c-7.

If your church tends to make many anxious decisions, grade lower on this scale (1–4). If your church makes equally anxious decisions and non-anxious decisions give yourself a 5, and if your church makes more non-anxious decisions than anxious decisions give your church a higher grade

(6–10). Think of staff hires, budgets, programs, ministries, committee members, outreaches, etc.

| — 1 — 2 — 3 — 4 — 5 — 6 — 7 — 8 — 9 — 10 — |

6. **Non-anxious churches aren't looking for the next best thing.** Philippians 4:8.

What do we focus on? If it's "true, noble, right, pure, lovely, admirable, excellent, and praiseworthy," grade yourself a 5–10. If it is another anxious way of pursuing our own platform and glory, attendance or budget, grade yourself a 1–5.

| — 1 — 2 — 3 — 4 — 5 — 6 — 7 — 8 — 9 — 10 — |

7. **Non-anxious churches are natural learners.** Philippians 4:9.

How comfortable is your church at networking with other churches? Not just the pastors getting together, but actually mixing your people together?

| — 1 — 2 — 3 — 4 — 5 — 6 — 7 — 8 — 9 — 10 — |

How willing are you to learn from other churches around you? Or are you a bit more concerned about if you would look like copy-cats or knockoffs?

| — 1 — 2 — 3 — 4 — 5 — 6 — 7 — 8 — 9 — 10 — |

8. **Non-anxious churches aren't alarmed by a little mess.** Philippians 4:10–11.

How frustrated does it make your leaders/pastors when the church service isn't perfect, when technology or people mess up? 1—Really frustrated. 10—It's all good, mistakes happen.

| — 1 — 2 — 3 — 4 — 5 — 6 — 7 — 8 — 9 — 10 — |

Appendix 1

How good is your church at saying "I'm sorry" and "I forgive you."? Is there a culture of fear to make mistakes? (1)

$$|-1-2-3-4-5-6-7-8-9-10-|$$

9. **Non-anxious churches learn to be content.** Philippians 4:11–13.

Would you say your church is content with how things currently are? If the church doesn't grow in numbers or budget? Or does that make the leaders and pastors nervous?

$$|-1-2-3-4-5-6-7-8-9-10-|$$

10. **Non-anxious churches live in the tension of diversity.** Philippians 1:27, 2:2–4, 3:2–3, 4:2.

How diverse would you say your church is? 10 being very diverse and 1 being not at all. Diversity includes not just skin colors or cultural backgrounds but also political beliefs, theological beliefs (doctrine and opinions), socio-economic, etc.

$$|-1-2-3-4-5-6-7-8-9-10-|$$

How comfortable is your church in that diversity? If they are secretly hoping or pushing for one way, then you need to grade your church lower.

$$|-1-2-3-4-5-6-7-8-9-10-|$$

RESULTS

Now, add it all up and see how your church did. Put your total score here _____.

125–150—Very non-anxious church.
105–125—On the track towards becoming a non-anxious church.
75–105—Trending towards a non-anxious church but a good amount of work left to do.
45–75—Trending towards an anxious church with a lot of work to do.
15–45—Very anxious church.

You should know that if you graded seventy-five or lower, there are going to be some really tough decisions in front of you. If you want to know how or where, the answer is above you. Take the lowest scores and work on those first. I would recommend working through this book and quiz with other leaders and influencers in your church. It's one of the most practical things you can do to become a more non-anxious church. Discuss each chapter and gather thoughts from trusted fellow co-laborers in the church. This also creates buy-in for the process, and ideally more people who are becoming non-anxious presences. The very act of reading this book slowly, patiently, and expectantly with feedback and vulnerability alongside others is itself an expression of non-anxiousness. Take those results and head back to chapter 8 to create a plan with the key leaders and decision-makers of your church and denomination to chart a path forward.

Finally, be grateful for both the big and small ways you see God working. Even if there are no noticeable changes, it would help to list the ways God is working in your church. Keep this list in front of you and in front of your church. Gratitude and anxiousness can't hang out together and so keep gratitude upfront as much as possible.

Acknowledgments

THIS PROJECT WAS STIRRED to life out of many conversations, life experiences, and soul-searching moments. I continuously began to see the church as a living body that also could be given to anxiousness and stress. The wrestling through spiritual formation in myself and in the church gave birth to this book. There are so many people behind a project like this, too many to even adequately mention in a small section titled "Acknowledgements." Anyone along the way in my journey with and in the church helped shape this book.

A huge thank you goes out to Wipf and Stock and their belief in this book. They saw the merit in it and believed it should be published. I was praying there would be a publisher that would give it a chance and I'm blessed it was Matthew Wimer and his team.

There were others along the way who continued to spur me along when I was ready to throw in the towel. Specifically, some strangers who became friends. I think of Beth Gaede who saw the potential in the project and even in me, gave me good advice and insight. Pete Ford was another one along the way who continued to encourage me and saw insights in the proposal that helped me get to Wipf and Stock. He was holding the map when I was feeling a bit lost.

This book comes from the support of a church that loves and encourages their pastor. They took a risk on a young pastor and I am so glad they did. Praise Covenant, you continue to lighten my load and uplift my spirits especially as I see you grow to be "with Jesus and like Jesus." Let's continue to grow together in the strength and goodness of Christ. To the staff that I get to partner on this journey, I am so grateful for you — Rick, Meredith, Aubrey, Laura, Ruth, Peter, and Lance. You are a blessing. Let's continue to be formed in the non-anxious way, the way of Jesus.

Acknowledgments

There is one particular group of people that I owe a deep debt of gratitude for this book. It's those first readers. When I began to compile chapters and an early rough draft, I didn't know what to expect. I took a leap of faith and shared it with you and your feedback, support, and encouragement enabled me to press on, "It's a book worth writing" — this was huge! Thank you; Adam, Nick, Aubrey, John, Brett, Mark, and my parents.

It was my family of origin that helped form much of how I see the church and my hope and desire for it to be healthy. I love you Mom and Dad, Jenny, and Ryan — couldn't have asked for a better family to be raised in.

To my friends that I love hanging out with, even if some of you could be better at returning text messages. I still love you. Thank you for being my friends; Tom, Tyler, Jon, Sam, Eddie, Drew, and so many others.

To the two people who made this dream a reality. Without your influence or help on this project it would be dead. There's no doubt in my mind that is true. Joan Smith, you are the salt of the earth — this project has your fingerprints all over it. I am so grateful for you. Mark Novak, I have learned so much from you and continue to do so. It was your view of the book that helped me finish it. Thank you for writing the forward. I am overjoyed by your words.

There is one final group of people that needs to be thanked even though they probably will never read these words. It's those who have given up on the church, but not on Jesus. I know some of you personally and when I see you around town, I am spurred on to get this book into pastors' and church leaders' hands. I hope you fall in love with the church again. I'm sorry that the anxious way of the church has pushed you away.

To the anchor in my life; my wonderful wife. I love you. I wouldn't have had the courage or discipline to write a book without your influence in my life. You've also helped me see the church in a way that is non-anxious. I am so glad for your strength and compassion in my life. Thank you for the three little ones we get to raise together. Kinsley, Cayson, Bridger, may you grow up with a new vision for the church. I am excited for you to grow in your faith and watch you discover the way of Jesus fully in your lives. I am already learning so much from you.

Finally, thank you, God, for the gift of these words and the ability to write them. While I lost some sleep at night as you gave me new insights and words to write in this book, I pray they may be pleasing to you and in a big or small way to help the church grow to be the resilient and beautiful bride of Christ.

Grace upon grace.

About Mark Knight

MARK KNIGHT is the Lead Pastor of Praise Covenant Church in Tacoma, WA. He has been married to his wife Lindsay for 13 years and they together have three beautiful children. He has an MDiv from North Park Theological Seminary and a BA from Northwest University. He loves to read, play golf, eat good food, and make people laugh all while pursuing a life cultivated by his time with Jesus so he can be more like Jesus.

CONTINUE THE CONVERSATION

🎧 Non-Anxious Churches Podcast

✉ nonanxiouschurches@gmail.com

Bibliography

Acuff, Jon. "*Fame Sucks*." acuff.me/fame-sucks/.
Alcoholics Anonymous. "*Alcoholics Anonymous 12 Steps*." 1981, www.aa.org/assets/en_US/smf-121_en.pdf.
Anonymous, "*Ambition*." Analogy Metaphor Creative Writing, www.metamia.com/analogize.php?q=ambition
Bolsinger, Tod E. *Tempered Resilience: How Leaders Are Formed in the Crucible of Change*. Downers Grover, IL: InterVarsity, 2020.
Bonhoeffer, Dietrich. *Cost of Discipleship*. SCM, London: 2015.
Bryan-Smith, James. Interview by Emily P. Freeman. "*Decision-Making with James Bryan-Smith*." The Next Right Thing Podcast. June 11, 2019. https://emilypfreeman.com/podcast/86/
Collier, Winn. *A Burning in My Bones: The Authorized Biography of Eugene H. Peterson*. Colorado Springs, CO: WaterBrook, 2021.
Comer, John Mark. *Different, Harder, Longer, Better: Waiting Well for Your Dreams to Come to Pass*. 2021. https://static1.squarespace.com/static/58431a7603596e3099e87531/t/60b83109724a9d3ed790ccee/1622683961986/Different%2C+Harder%2C+Longer%2C+Better+-+Waiting+well+for+your+dreams+to+come+to+pass
Charles, H. B., Jr. *On Pastoring: A Short Guide to Living, Leading, and Ministering as a Pastor*. Chicago: Moody, 2016.
Dickson, John. *Bullies and Saints: An Honest Look at the Good and Evil of Christian History*. Grand Rapids, MI: Zondervan, 2021.
DeGroat, Chuck. *When Narcissism Comes to Church*. Downers Grove, IL: InterVarsity, 2020.
Du Mez, Kristin Kobes. *Jesus and John Wayne: How White Evangelicals Corrupted a Faith and Fractured a Nation*. New York: Liveright, 2020.
Dude, You're Screwed. "*African Ambush*." Season 2, Episode 02, NBC, 10, February. 2015.
Gonzalez, Justo L. *Santa Biblia: The Bible Through Hispanic Eyes*. Nashville, TN: Abingdon, 1996.
Gossai, Hemchand. "*Steward*." In *The Eerdmans Bible Dictionary*, 1252. Grand Rapids, MI: Eerdmans, 2000.
Hawthorne, Gerald F., and Ralph P. Martin, eds. *Dictionary of Paul and His Letters*. Downers Grove, IL: InterVarsity, 1993.
Jethani, Skye. *With: Reimagining the Way You Relate to God*. Nashville, TN: Thomas Nelson, 2011.

Bibliography

Lawrence, Brother. *Practicing the Presence of God: A Modernized Christian Classic.* Brewster, MA: Paraclete, 2007.

Lewis, C. S. *Mere Christianity.* New York: Simon and Schuster, 1996.

Louw, J. P., and E. A. Nida. *Greek-English Lexicon of the New Testament: Based on Semantic Domains* (electronic ed. of the 2nd edition). New York: United Bible Societies, 1996.

McAllister, Cameron, and Stuart McAllister. *Faith That Lasts: A Father and Son on Cultivating Lifelong Belief.* Downers Grove, IL: InterVarsity, 2020.

McKnight, Scot, and Laura Barringer. *A Church Called Tov: Forming a Goodness Culture That Resists Abuses of Power and Promotes Healing.* Carol Stream, IL: Momentum, 2020.

Mcleod, Saul. "*Robbers Cave Experiment.*" Robbers Cave Experiment / Realistic Conflict Theory | Simply Psychology, 1 Jan. 1970, www.simplypsychology.org/robbers-cave.html.

Meier, Mattheisen SM, et al. "Increased Mortality Among People with Anxiety Disorders: Total Population Study." Br J Psychiatry 209.3 (2016) 216–21.

Nave, Orville J., and Edward Viening. *The New Nave's Topical Bible.* Grand Rapids, MI: Zondervan, 1983.

Newbell, Trillia. *United: Captured by God's Vision for Diversity.* Chicago: Moody, 2014.

Nouwen, Henri. *The Selfless Way of Christ: Downward Mobility and the Spiritual Life.* Ossining, NY: Orbis, 2011.

———. *The Wounded Healer: Ministry in Contemporary Society.* New York: Image, 1979.

Peterson, Eugene H. *A Long Obedience in the Same Direction: Discipleship in an Instant Society.* Downers Grove, IL: InterVarsity, 2000.

Sarah, Cardinal Robert, and Nicolas Diat. *The Power of Silence: Against the Dictatorship of Noise.* San Francisco: Ignatius, 2017.

Sherif, Muzafer. "*Experiments in Group Conflict.*" Scientific American 195.5, 1956, pp. 54–58.

———. *Intergroup Conflict and Cooperation: The Robbers Cave Experiment.* Whitefish, MT: Literary Licensing, 2013.

Sivers, Derek. "*How to Start a Movement.*" Ted Talk, Youtube, 1 Apr. 2010, www.youtube.com/watch?v=V74AxCqOTvg&t=51s.

Spurgeon, Charles. "*The Anxious Inquirer.*" In *Spurgeon's Sermon.* Peabody, MA: Hendrickson, 2020.

Starke, John. Twitter post. April 20, 2021, 12:16pm. https://twitter.com/john_starke/status/1384586679785299968

Swenson, Richard A. *Margin: Restoring Emotional, Physical, Financial, and Time Reserves to Overloaded Lives.* Colorado Springs, CO: NavPress, 2004.

The Office. "*The Job.*" Season 3, Episode 23, NBC, 17 May, 2007.

Villodas, Rich. *The Failure of Celebrity Christianity.* Qideas, YouTube, 23 Apr. 2021, www.youtube.com/watch?v=82U8Cz5TSsw.

Warren, Harrison Tish. *Prayer in the Night: for Those Who Work or Watch or Weep.* Downers Grove, IL: InterVarsity, 2021.

Willard, Dallas. *The Divine Conspiracy: Rediscovering Our Hidden Life in God.* New York: HarperOne, 1998.

———. *Renovation of the Heart: Putting on the Character of Christ - 10th Anniversary Edition.* Colorado Springs, CO: NavPress, 2012.

Wilson, Andrew. "*Do Not Worry.*" Sermon, 2015. www.youtube.com/watch?v=c1RDUYADYK4

www.ingramcontent.com/pod-product-compliance
Lightning Source LLC
Chambersburg PA
CBHW050824160426
43192CB00010B/1883